0901 2

D1632669

THE COUNTRYMAN
Companion

Edited by Richard Askwith

An occasional publication

First published in Great Britain 2002 by
Countryman Publishing Limited
23 Sheep Street, Burford, Oxfordshire OX18 4LS
© Countryman Publishing Limited

A British Cataloguing in Publication record
is available for this book
ISBN 0 9543993 0 7

All rights reserved. This book must not be circulated in any form of
binding or cover other than that in which it is published and without
similar condition of this being imposed on the subsequent purchaser.
No part of this publication may be reproduced, stored on a retrieval
system or transmitted in any form, or by any means, electronic,
mechanical, photocopying, recording or otherwise, without either
prior permission in writing from the publisher or a licence permitting
restricted copying. In the United Kingdom such licences are issued by
the Copyright Licensing Agency, 90 Tottenham Court Road, London,
W1P 9AH. The right of Peter Ackroyd, Neal Ascherson, Richard
Askwith, Annalisa Barbieri, David Bellamy, Piers Browne, Nathalie
Curry, Duff Hart-Davis, Frederick Forsyth, Max Hastings, Hester Lacey,
Richard Mabey, Andrew Motion, Alice Oswald, Jonathan Roberts,
Peggy Vance and David Walker to be identified as authors of this work
has been asserted in accordance with the Copyright Designs and
Patents Acts 1988.

Printed by Smith Settle, Otley

Contents

Illustrations

Editor's note

THERE HAS BEEN MUCH SAID AND WRITTEN THIS YEAR BY people, especially politicians, claiming to speak on behalf of 'rural folk'. But as those who live and work in the countryside know, those 'rural folk' have always come in different shapes and sizes – and all think differently. In 21st century Britain they are more diverse than ever, from the dwindling minority who have worked all their lives on the land to the growing host of newcomers, commuters, itinerants and visitors who connect to their countryside and its traditions in other ways and for other reasons – differently, but no less passionately.

This collection of writing and illustration on rural themes is a celebration of that diversity: a range of contrasting voices from a variety of generations and points of view, all united by one peculiarly British quality: a sense of humble wonder at the inexhaustible complexities of our precious land.

RICHARD ASKWITH

ANDREW MOTION

While I was fishing

"DO YOU WANT TO…" AND SOMETIMES "WOULD YOU LIKE TO…" my mother sang, never sure which was right. "Do you want to swing on a star? Carry moonbeams home in a jar?" I was six but I knew what she meant. I had these friends, the Routledge twins: Andrew and Peter. My own two Christian names, but divided up like that I didn't recognise them as mine. Andrew was quiet and cautious, Peter quick and reckless. They lived nearby. You turned out of the village along a concrete track which ran flat for half a mile under a splintery ash-canopy, then plunged downhill between giant clapboard barns, over a brick bridge and – woah! – ended in a gate overlooking a field with a bull in it.

The day I'm thinking about, Peter led us from the house to the bridge, and Andrew and I dropped down after him on to the river bank. Peter was carrying a jam jar with a string round the neck. They were wearing blue boiler suits, walking ahead of me in Indian file, all of us as silent as we could be, but our boots squeaking on the shiny grass. We reached a place where the bank dipped in a clump of alder trees. Last year's seed cones were still there like miniature pineapples, and when we lay flat they pressed hard into us. The world was shrunken and huge at once: monstrous ants tetchily going about whatever business we had disturbed; a loopy spider legging it from blade to blade. When had I last taken a breath? Not since the bridge, not a proper one, and I wasn't going to start now.

Peter was working forward on his elbows like a commando – we all were – hanging his head over the lip of the bank. A crumbling orange cliff, thin alder roots poking out, Peter's hand already in the water, and the blood thundering into our brains. It wasn't a river, really, it was a stream – 3-4ft across, with a sandy bottom which made the water look brown, even though it was clear. Too narrow for anything, I thought, too small – except there below me, wobbling in the current, was a fish as big as my forearm. "Chub," mouthed Andrew, his lips making a soft pop. The way sunlight was falling, I couldn't see Peter's hand in the water any more, but I knew it must be sliding up behind the fish, perhaps even touching him, stroking him so he thought there was no danger. Then came the trashing hoist and the fish in mid-air – just for a second – the yellow eye glaring, the green-blue body curved inside its crescent of water-drops. Then another second as it straightened and started to fall. Then another second as it slapped into the stream and melted.

In a while, Peter caught some sticklebacks under the bridge, and a miller's thumb. Because I had just seen the chub like that – beautiful and by itself in mid-air – I didn't expect them to look much. But they were miraculous. The sticklebacks (three spines not 10) with their medieval spikes and scarlet belly-smudge. The armour-plated miller's thumb. Peter filled his jam jar with water, slid them inside, and gave them to me to take home. Moonbeams home in a jar. No, not moonbeams. Bits of the moon itself, but dark.

We were staying at a lodge in the Cairngorms, and walking down to the river in the early morning my mother and I passed the stable where dead stags were hung up by their heels. The door stood half open. Metal buckets shone under their heads, catching the blood-drips. A man was in there, whistling but out of sight. My mother's dog, however – she'd come along: a second-hand collie called Beauty. Beauty squirted ahead then sidled back grinning as we tramped through a belt of spruce to the river bank. My mother had forgotten the leash but it didn't matter. We weren't going to catch anything. She was 5ft 9in, and thin, and often ill, and easily tired. None of that mattered either. It was all in the timing. You see? She paid out her line into the water, letting the current take the fly round 45 degrees, then began lifting her rod, slowly at first then accelerating, stopping it just above the vertical so the line flew out behind in a dripping skirl, then propelling it forward, light as a cobweb on the river, the fly just short of the far bank, already ferrying through the current. "You try. You'll soon get the hang of it." But of course I didn't, not that day. After 20 minutes of picking my fly from the trees behind me, from the grass, stooping over the reel with its spaghetti-fall of tangled line, she took over again.

It's 35 years ago, and I've forgotten how the fish took, how soon. I can still see it though, as it began to flag and my mother drew it towards her: one minute clear brown racing water, then a spangle of light-fragments like big fishscales, then a silver ingot, rigid and heavy, then an iron jaw stuck out. When it found me and the dog looming over the bank, all its energy came back like a thunderbolt, the silver etherising at once, the water empty, my mother cursing. Which meant another eternity of waiting – but back at the edge of the trees this time, hanging on to the dog by its collar. There were supposed to be golden eagles nearby, and I thought if I concentrated on looking for them, it would soon be over. I searched the sky minutely, the sun coming clear of cloud then slipping away, and eventually breaking into trickles and streams and blotches. The gorgeous taut fish was assembling itself from the broken pieces of the world – gravel, wind, water, sun. It was fixing its bony mind on death, and rising towards me steadily.

My friend and I parked in the lee of a barn, already not talking, pulled on our waders in the moonlight, and stomped off through the churned-up gateway as though we could see exactly where we were going. The Torridge is a beautiful river, running off Exmoor into the sea by Bideford. It was clear enough when we got there – the moon skidding through ragged cloud, a herd of half-visible Friesians frisking at a distance and breathing mightily. My friend climbed in first, and when he had fished downriver for a while I waded in behind. The extraordinary feeling that you're about to get soaked – your skin prickling and lungs empty – but only the waders tightening against you! Thigh-deep here, no more, and the bottom firm when I left the clay-slumps under the bank. And alders plaited together overhead, so casting was difficult. After a few yards and no problems, the universe began to expand and settle. Black water pressing flat against the back of my legs. The Friesians forgetting us and shuffling into a huddle. Bats nipping round a tall ash. Moonlight flickering on the river, on my friend's shoulders ahead of me, on my line sizzling backwards as it drew its sparkling signature then stiffened forward and lay down silently.

It took an hour to fish the beat through – more, since we were dawdling – and after the first few minutes I already knew there was nothing. My friend knew it too. In a few minutes we would find a way along the bank upriver and climb in somewhere else. But while we were here, why didn't we fish it through once more, just to be sure? This time I go first. The bats, peeping on their radar. And that sloppy cascade must be the cows. But really everything is the river, its immense slow tonnage bearing down on me. That's not why I am crouching forward, though. It's not even because at this angle I can see my fly slipping in under the low bushes and round the difficult boulders. I am bending close to everything because I think if I keep going like this I might have my vision. I might see all the fish in the river swivelling towards me, all on a collision course but all missing me, like it is when you're driving through snow, and headlights put you at the exact centre of the universe, and each individual flake comes straight for you then goes, comes straight for you then goes.

Some time after my mother's death I am reading Aksakov. He is pike fishing at night, on the track of an old mill-monster, and a fire is stoked in the small grate amid-ships. Yellow flame-light pours off the oarsmen and the spearsman. He is, he tells me, in "some sort of half-conscious state, combined (I must admit) with a certain amount of fear". Later he is "certain that hunters were the first to begin creating the world of myth that exists among all peoples". I know what he is saying. He means what happens to my head during the hours alone, with the water making and unmaking itself, with my line flicking ahead and back, with the ripples and little waves opening and closing, giving their glimpse of what I half-see, half-imagine. He means that mood when she is still alive. When the air around me is soft and shimmering. When the mind is intent but easy. When words form out of nowhere. Alder cones and midges and nettle flowers flipping into the water. Glittering shock-rings. The heart ripening in its excitement, entranced, believing the whole of its past has come within reach and is catchable.

My father and I went for a week on the River Dee in Scotland. We shared a rod, so when I was in the water he waited on the bank – on the close-cropped grass, with the pine-woods wheezing sleepily behind him. I was fishing a wide elbow, and when I'd been through the bend, and looked back at him, he was closer than before, though I felt he'd been moving away. He was lounging under a green oak tree, the smoke from his cigarette wibbling straight up to heaven. It was a crisp day, and we were doing what we wanted, but he looked hollow. He was daydreaming about my mother, dead for 20 years but unfading, today wearing her waders and silver-brown tweed hat with its whiskery band of flies.

I turned back to the river, crouching forward, and the dazzle began streaming at me again. This time it wasn't snow flakes, it was faces. The miniature faces of the dead.

Some undulating through the white air, some skimming among the mayflies, some within the water, fighting the current so their hair streamed out behind them, their mouths opened, and their lips pressed thin and white against their teeth. I cast into them again and again, bringing up nothing. Bringing up nothing until a salmon rose in front of me. The whole dark circle of its pool shuddered. Another moment of nothing. Another. But all that time the salmon was quietly gathering itself, sensing something, swinging away from me under the bank so it brushed a fall of bramble, then linking towards me again just as my fly landed on the spot it had left. When it drew level with me, exactly level, it leaped clean out of the water, shoulder-high. Leaping for pure joy, I thought, my heart lifting. I had it fixed in mid-air, free and separate from everything else in the world, but belonging to me and me alone: the burnished silver back, the strenuous tail spreadeagled, the shocking pale belly and the warrior head. I was a child again, staring into the hard yellow eye. I was as old as my father dreaming in the shade. Then that long second ended and the fish was beyond me, slapping down through the surface and disappearing. Charging on towards the mountains and the stony headwaters.

Andrew Motion's new collection of poetry and prose, Public Property *(in which this article appears), is published by Faber & Faber (£12.99).*

FREDERICK FORSYTH

View from the March

THERE ARE ONLY TWO REASONS, ON THIS EARTH, WHY things happen: Act of God and Act of Man. We all know about the first – the volcano, the earthquake, the tornado. Natural disasters, unpredictable, unpreventable. Act of Man accounts for 99 per cent of things that affect us daily, and subdivides in two. Inadvertent and intended. When things go badly wrong and the cause is incompetence, however sheer, however blithering, as with the handling of the foot-and-mouth disaster, we call it the Cock-up Theory. But sometimes things go wrong through deliberate malignity. That is when the clever dicks pooh-pooh the so-called Conspiracy Theory as mere paranoia. But it is not always paranoia. Some things go badly wrong through planned malice. Thus it is, I believe, with the British countryside. One has only to listen to the utter contempt with which Tony Blair regards rustics (remember his 'tally-ho' sneer?) or the naked hatred with which John Prescott views country folk. The proof lies in a single question, never asked by our pretty tame media, quite unanswerable by any Labour politician. It is this. Given that we Brits are surrounded by the Irish, French, Dutch and Danes; given that we all farm under the same sky, in the same latitudes, with the same climate and under the same EU rules; how come all our neighbours prosper in contentment while we are bankrupt, unviable, with never-ceasing tales of yet another suicide from rank despair? The reason no Labour politician can answer that is because there is but one answer. Act of Man, meaning national government. Ah, say the apologists, but that is because New Labour does not understand the countryside.

Poppycock. Attlee, Gaitskell, Wilson, Callaghan, they all led Labour Parties that never saw any reason to persecute the countryside and the people in it. Anyway, it has been more than five years. If you come to power and there is something that eludes you, you get the best experts you can find, ask them and listen. Problem solved. No, the difference is that Ireland, France, Holland, Denmark, under Conservative or Social Democrat regimes, would never play host to the sheer venom, the vitriol, the vindictiveness that informs British Labour in its class hatred. (All country people, even the humblest, are included as 'toffs' in Labour's class hatred.)

More proof? Consider this. Supposing jumping on a horse in a pink coat and chasing a fox was the traditional weekend recreation of the British working class. Supposing going to the lake or reservoir with rod, line, hook and worm was what country-dwelling Middle England did. How far would the anti-hunting campaign have proceeded by now? Not one inch, and we all know it, including Tony Blair and John Prescott. The anti-hunting campaign is 80 per cent class hatred fuelled, 20 per cent fox concern, zero per cent first-hand knowledge. But the hostility in Labour to the entire countryside, lock, stock and barrel, is more complex. Basically it stems not from bewildered ignorance (a time-raddled excuse) but from a conviction that the people of the landscape simply do not fit in to the matrix of Blair's New Britain in the one-party, no opposition, post-democratic age.

Add that to the proven conviction (the 'forces of conservatism' speech) that any form of opposition or even disagreement must not simply be beaten at the polls but annihilated, and you have September's 'Liberty and Livelihood' march in context. The march that I saw was traditional Britain trying to make a point; what have we done wrong, why can't you leave us alone, why do you use every possible legal, bureaucratic, financial and economic weapon to beat us with? Like traditional Britain, it was cheerful, well-mannered, orderly, tolerant and tidy. I watched the Met police officers, 1,600 and completely unnecessary, marvelling at the contrast with their usual duties during demonstrations. But will it work? Will 400,000 Brits on the streets of the capital cause a sea change in Downing Street's attitude? That is where I come adrift from the leadership of the Countryside Alliance, in the form of three committed Labour supporters. My own view is: not a cat in hell's chance. Why?

I have studied the Blairite government with some intensity for over five years. Unlike many inside the London 'circuit' I do not seek their company, their confidences, their promotions, their favours, their money, their tip-offs, their interviews or their honours. I do not need to bow the knee, mince words. In my view this government has demonstrated three overriding characteristics, apart from administrative incompetence. First, it is a liar government. It lies as it breathes. We have been lied to over the Dome, devolution, Europe, Railtrack, dodgy donations, the euro, hospital waiting-lists... you name it. As I write, the lies are about A-levels and hunting. But the most cynical of all was the blatant lie that it would make the scrupulously impartial Burns Report the cornerstone of policy. Two, it is a bully. Time and again the most harmless critics have been character-assassinated to beat them into submission. This was even tried on the mild Lord Tommy Burns because he could not say what they wanted him to say.

Finally, it is a coward, and this is its only Achilles heel at the moment. It has shown that it only appeases the perceived greater danger to itself. A no-threat critic can simply be crushed. For years it has feared the power to hurt it posed by the fanaticism, ruthlessness and money of the 'sabby' lobby, RSPCA, LACS, IFAW, PETA and Political Animal Lobby. Plus the 200-250 class-hatred-fuelled backbenchers. The Countryside Alliance has been smiled at, invited to another conference, offered a moderate compromise (always withdrawn), patted and petted. We have had one rally in Hyde Park and two massive marches. We might as well have peed in the Atlantic to try to raise the temperature. In the inner councils of Labour the CA is despised as harmless; amiable blowhards, Colonel Blimps, not politically dangerous in terms of lost seats, legal harassment, concerted anti-Labour militancy. I absolutely repudiate illegal violence, but the idea that six million angry country folk are just a bag of hot air is an idea that has got to change, and change now. If not, will the last farmer in Britain turn off the light when he leaves?

HESTER LACEY

The wisdom of bees

RECENTLY OUR NEIGHBOUR JIM, FROM A FEW DOORS DOWN the hill, kindly offered us an old hive. Jim, a retired science teacher, has been keeping bees for more than a decade. His honey has won prizes. He came round to supper a few days ago with a jar for us, plus a pair of enormous artichokes from his garden. The honeycomb, rich brown rather than golden, had been plunked unceremoniously into an old jam jar, but the taste was sublime. Jim reckons we could get up to 60lb of honey from just one hive next spring. So now one of his hives is standing behind our house, waiting to be cleaned, renovated, and made weatherproof and cosy. It's a job for the winter and it needs to be finished without fail, because next spring I'm preparing to add several thousand extra members to my household...

I've been fascinated by bees, albeit from a distance, for about 25 years. I did a project on them in primary school, and, as a conscientious child, added a copy of the *Ladybird Book of Bees* to my bookshelf. The book has gone missing over the years. I know, however, that what caught my imagination at the age of nine or 10 was its description of the waggle dance. Bees that find a tempting crop of flowers hasten back to the hive to tell their friends. They shimmy over the combs, and the way they dance tells the other bees where to collect the food. I devoted a whole page of my project book to a drawing of a rickety web of hexagons, representing the comb, with a fat, smiling, stripy bee on them, and thick black arrows to show the way he was wiggling around.

Beekeeping when we lived in London never seemed a good idea. Keeping bees is certainly quite possible in cities, but you do need space, and a tiny patio by Clapham Junction station won't do. And, though the time commitment isn't huge, you do need to be around. No living creatures, except perhaps goldfish, fit in round an office day topped and tailed with a long commute. You can't breeze in late at night, leave early in the morning, and hope everything will tick over: this doesn't even work with plants. An optimistic scheme to grow tomatoes in growbags on our Clapham roof was a miserable failure and posed a clear and present danger to passers-by in the shape of plummeting rotten fruit.

This summer, two years after quitting Clapham for north Dorset, we have our own tomatoes at last, grown more sensibly at ground level in a proper greenhouse. Our first year was spent establishing order inside our cottage; now we've had time to turn our attention to the garden. And this summer – another landmark – I had my first proper look inside a living hive. I was invited over by Liz, doyenne and secretary of the local beekeepers' association. We made endless appointments to meet at her house, which then had to be broken, because it was drizzling, or rainy, or because it simply looked as though it might turn wet. Bees are only approachable in settled weather; rain makes them tetchy. Finally, one Saturday was judged cloudy but hopeful. I was supposed to be driving over alone: my husband was initially dubious about the whole undertaking (as he was about our move to Dorset, then the dog, then the vegetable garden, and then the chickens, who will be arriving next spring). But I cadged a lift from him, and when we arrived and he was enthusiastically offered the loan of a suit he didn't like to refuse. So we saw our first comb of live bees together.

Liz and her husband Alan, both retired, started keeping bees 20 years ago, quite by chance. Alan was out gardening when a great cloud of bees came swarming through the air. They settled in a derelict old hive by a nearby barn. A beekeeping friend who came over to collect it was rather daunted by the size of the swarm. Liz and Alan decided to hang on to half. "We were manhandling this great mass of bees, without even having suits," recalls Liz. "I was holding a piece of wood against the hive to keep them in – completely foolish. Once we'd got them into our garden, I went on a course – quite the wrong way of doing things: you should learn about the bees before you get them. I remember," she adds thoughtfully, "one chap on the course got stung on the nose one week, then the next week he was stung again in exactly the same place."

After two decades, Liz still treats her bees with great respect. "I'm still learning," she says. "You never stop. If you ask different people they give you different advice, they all have totally different views. The books all say different things too. And the bees don't always read the same books as you do, and will sometimes surprise you by doing something funny." We zipped ourselves carefully into protective suits and lumbered slowly towards the hives – nine of them, set against the far hedge of the gardens, well beyond the banks of flowers and neat ranks of vegetables. Although the suits are very lightweight, the extra layer doesn't make for grace – and sudden movements are one of the (various) things bees find annoying.

Liz, fair and pink-cheeked, is bustling, brisk, friendly and efficient, as befits her role as society secretary. But when she approached her hives, all her movements slowed right down, until she was not so much walking as calmly gliding. Reaching the front door of the first hive, she puffed smoke into it. Smoke scares the bees into believing that a fire is threatening the hive, so they stuff themselves with honey, in case they have to flee and leave their stores behind; full stomachs make bees slower and more docile, much like humans. Then she lifted off the lid of the hive. When the wooden roof comes off, the honeycombs are the first section you reach. Lifted out on their wooden frames, each with its cargo of live workers, they are mesmerising and beautiful. The light catches the facets on the bees' wings as they move over the comb and makes them glitter; the mass of individuals slides over the wax cells like water in perpetual motion. The mesh of a beekeeper's veil is very fine, and becomes invisible when it is 6in from the eyes, which is roughly where it sits when the hat's on your head. The first sight of a comb of live bees is enough to make you step back, forgetting for a minute that there's anything between you and them. And they do buzz in close to inspect you. You don't casually flick a bee from your veil in case you brush the netting so close to your face that she can sting; you have to ignore the inquisitive one clinging inches from your nose.

The queen bee, longer-bodied and larger than the rest, is kept in the bottom section of the hive by a separator, a wire grille that she's too plump to squeeze through. Here she lays eggs in hexagonal cells just like those that the workers store the honey in, and the workers tend the growing larvae. In Liz's hive, every time we saw a fat, furry drone we thought we'd spotted the queen. The drones are the male bees; their sole purpose in life is to mate with virgin queen bees. On a queen's maiden flight, she might mate with 15 or 20 drones, and from this all the eggs she will lay in her whole lifetime are fertilised. The drones can sense when queens from other hives nearby are setting out on their mating flight, and head off lustily to join the orgy. Other than that, all they do is eat. A hedonistic life, until the autumn, when they are all slung out to die of cold and starvation; greedy drones would be a drain on food resources over the colder months.

Liz eventually picked out the queen, half-hidden in a knot of workers. (Many beekeepers mark their queens with a tiny spot of paint on their backs, so they can easily be picked out of the crowd.) Then, after half an hour, the bees started fidgeting around us more persistently and ominously; the hum from the hive rose a decibel or two. Liz said that they were getting agitated, that the weather must be changing, and that it was time to leave them in peace. Sure enough, on our way home, it began to rain heavily. However, that first half hour had been enough to hook us both. We bought a pair of second-hand suits so we could go to the regular meetings of our local bee group, held at a different hive every few weeks through the summer. Other members include farmers, gardeners, retired folk, and a younger couple who've just started their own organic smallholding.

As novices, we swathe ourselves impregnably from head to foot. Bees like to climb, and if one lands on you, clambers up and finds a chink in your armour, woe betide. And if you're stung once, the other bees can sense it, and become alert to join in the attack. Veteran beekeepers, however, will confidently handle the frames in which the bees build their combs without gloves, or even veil. Watching David, the chair of the society, slowly lift out a frame bare-handed had me shifting from foot to foot, nervously murmuring: "He's forgotten his gloves! Shouldn't we tell him?" David, however, laughs benignly at such concern. "If you're gentle with them, chances are they'll be gentle with you," he says. "I've been called out by lots of people with nasty bees, and then they say 'Oh, they're not nasty with you'. You have to be slow and gentle, and when you move the first frame, give them the chance to get out of the way. They don't like being crushed." Which is fair enough, surely. Some days, he says, a hive is easy to work on; other days, the bees are cross. It depends on the weather, and on getting to know the bees.

David has snow-white hair and a softly-spoken, quietly humorous manner: precise and gentle in the way that many beekeepers are. His house is called The Hive, and he has six of them in his back garden, living happily alongside his fat, friendly Khaki Campbell ducks. Before he kept bees, he was a skilled amateur lepidopterist, but he decided he had had enough of a hobby that ultimately led only to corpses pinned behind a frame. Bees filled the gap, and the atmosphere also proved congenial. "Bee groups and clubs are a really good mix of older people, youngsters, different ideas and ages and outlooks. You're never short of helping hands. Nobody wants to show off. The only time people might get a bit secretive about their technique is round the time of a honey show, but even then you'll ask them what they're doing and they'll most likely tell you."

He adds cheerfully that a sting or two is part and parcel, and that unless you're allergic to bee venom, it shouldn't bother you much. "The first sting you get at the beginning of the year swells up a bit. After that you don't get much of a reaction." Chopped mallow leaves, he says, are what you should dab on bee-stings. This year has been a very good year; David harvested 700lb of honey from his hives.

As well as honey, David makes mead, fruit wines sweetened with honey rather than sugar, furniture polish and traditional dipped candles. He sells much of it through the village shop. But over and above their honey yield, he feels genuine affection towards his quarter-of-a-million charges. "I've lost hives in the past and the great satisfaction is a good crop, then getting them through the winter and seeing them thrive in spring. It's very satisfying to see them nice and strong in spring. You don't realise how much you think of them until they get a disease." David has been keeping bees for around 15 years and had just started breeding his own queens, three years in, when his hives were infected with foul brood. "I lost three out of four hives. You have to pour petrol over the colonies and set them alight, and burn all your equipment too. Then it all has to be buried in a pit 3ft deep. It does knock you back. But you pick yourself up and start all over again."

David was immediately able to tell me that my proposed hive site was wrong. It was under trees, which will drip on the roof, and it is damp that carries off colonies in the winter, not cold. So we shall now be putting our hive 50 yards or so closer to the house. One hive will be plenty for us to start with; but an experienced beekeeper has less to do than a beginner. "Once you've been keeping bees some time, you don't need to look in the hive as often. If I can see plenty of bees flying, plenty of pollen going in, I know all's well." His bees, he says, will forage from the first snowdrops at the end of February, to the final ivy flowers in November. There are two crucial six-week periods where they lay down their surplus honey, one in spring, one in summer. Recently, a warm spring has often been followed by a cold June, and the bees have eaten up the honey they laid down in spring themselves. Bad signs for the honey harvest are a sudden desire for water – or an unexpected, ruthless cull of the drones. "If I see my bees collecting water from the pond to dilute the honey, or if they start chucking the drones out early, even throwing the drone grubs out of the cells, I know there's not much food going in."

The mystique of bees – how they communicate with each other and run their orderly communities – is as fascinating as the prospect of full golden jars. What's known of their social and domestic life is a hybrid of Elizabethan tragedy and science fiction. Ridley Scott's aliens, with their monstrous queen and uncanny knack of reading each other's minds, were based on insect colonies. Some scientists have even suggested that a hive of bees should not be regarded as thousands of individuals, but as a single entity. Jim – the neighbour who offered us his old hive – once put a tape-recorder into one of his hives on a day when he knew that a new queen was likely to be hatching.

This happens in the Spring, sometimes several times, sometimes not at all. When a swarm leaves the hive, it isn't led by a new queen with a band of young pioneers – it's the old queen, with a few faithful retainers, who's taking off. The old queen is deposed if she loses control of the colony, either because it has become too big or because the chemicals she exudes to keep the other bees in order are losing their potency. The workers then make perhaps a dozen or so special egg cells, larger and more luxurious than usual. The grubs from the eggs laid in them are fed exclusively on royal jelly secreted by the workers. All bee babies are fed on royal jelly for the first few days of their lives; but after that the worker larvae are switched to more prosaic fare of honey and pollen. Worker larvae grow to normal bee size and are sterile. The ones kept on the magical jelly diet grow bigger and become sexually mature. Then the first new queen hatches.

Jim played me the tape that captures that moment. First you hear the deep hum of the hive at work. Then there comes an eerie, high-pitched chirping – and the background noise of the thousands of busy workers drops away. They have frozen into silence as the first new queen begins to 'pipe'. She is seeking out her unhatched rivals. These will only be a few hours, maybe even minutes, from emerging themselves; but there is no second place in this race. Curled in their cells, they can't keep themselves from answering the piping queen, with a croaking sound known as 'quarking'. It's a fatal impulse. The newly-hatched queen rips open the cells where her sisters are quarking and tears their heads off. It's this kind of strange habit that makes bees such an enticing prospect. Imagine having all that going on at the bottom of the garden.

Jim is genial and bearded, and retains the traces of his native Shropshire accent. He originally took up beekeeping to get over his fear of stinging insects; now he is something of a bee boffin. He has started researching a PhD study into drone assemblies. These happen when large numbers of drones gather together in a vigorous, buzzing crowd, waiting for the arrival of queens on their mating flights. No one is sure how the drones' meeting points are decided; it may be something to do with the earth's magnetic field. But the drone assemblies, if undisturbed, continue in the same places for years, even centuries. Gilbert White recorded one at Selborne in 1779; when Jim went to have a look at the site over 200 years later, the drones were still gathering eagerly.

The most sensible way for us to acquire our first colony will be to hope some local friend finds a spring swarm that they want to pass on. That way we can be reasonably sure the bees don't have too ferocious a temperament (although crosser bees tend to be the most early-rising and hard-working, and thus produce the most honey). It also means that there'll be someone there to help us pick them up. Swarms that form early in the year tend to gather on low branches in trees or hedges. You turn up in full protective gear, position a box on a sheet strategically placed underneath the mass and gently sever the branch. Then you invert the box, wrap it all up in the sheet, and lug it into the back of the car. And then you drive home, at low speed, avoiding bumps in the road, introduce the bees to their new home, and wait to see what happens next.

RICHARD ASKWITH

Mud, toil, tears and sweat

SCAFELL PIKE, AN EARLY AFTERNOON IN JUNE. IT'S AS HOT as a crowded tube train, and yet somehow strands of thin cloud, carefully arranged, obscure all but the sharp rocks in front of me. My left ankle is a giant bruise, and I'm half-mad with thirst, but I daren't slow down for fear of losing touch with the pair of runners in front, perhaps 20 or 30 yards away. Once that happens, it's back to the map and compass, and everything will take twice as long. On the other hand, we've been running for an hour and a half already and, frankly, I've had enough.

No good even thinking of that. Once you start feeling sorry for yourself, you're finished. Or, rather, you're any-thing but finished, because you still have to get home, and the distances don't get any shorter when you give up. They just take longer. On this occasion – the Borrowdale Fell Race 2002 – I reckon we've done about seven out of the 17 miles, with Great Gable and Dale Head the only sig-nificant summits still to climb on the way back to

Rossthwaite. Funny how long it takes, though, on a day like this. Funny how the heat drains the strength from your legs. Funny how we haven't passed any streams recently. Funny how the very best runners are already probably three or four miles ahead. And funny how, every time I get lost in my thoughts, the next time I look the pair in front are further away.

We plunge down from the summit, suppressing every impulse of common sense to run freely across the slanting moonscape. It hurts, but by this stage it hurts if you walk, too. And, the faster you run on this kind of terrain, the less likely you are to twist or break an ankle. Conversely, you're more likely to fall off a cliff. But there's no time to think about that. Too busy looking at the rocks. Some walkers coming the other way glance at us indifferently: half the field will have passed them by now. None the less, one of them – a middle-aged man with a thin, intelligent face – catches my eye and seems to mouth a single, incredulous word: "Why?" It's a good question, but, of course, there's no time to think about that either. Take your mind off these rocks for more than a fraction of a second and you'll be flat on your face or worse. And any fractions of a second you *can* spare are needed for keeping an eye on the pair of runners ahead – who have now all but vanished.

"When you get to the scree on the Corridor Route," the race organiser announced to us at the start, "remember, it's very wet at the moment, and it's *dangerous*." Which is a pity, because (a) I hate all forms of mountain-related danger and (b) the scree on the Corridor Route is, I think, exactly where we're now headed. Oddly enough, despite years of fell-running in these parts, I've never previously used this route. I suspect I haven't missed much. True, it's a brilliantly direct way to get from the summit of Scafell Pike to the Sty Head saddle between Great End and Great Gable. But it's slippery and narrow and uncomfortably steep, and I'm pretty sure there's a ghastly drop somewhere to my left. Then we get to the scree slopes, and my spirits rise. Yes, the 'path' heads almost vertically down. Yes, it's a long, long way to the bottom. And, yes, if you once lost control it would be difficult to stop. But the stones are nice and small, and, in this stormy heat, they're not so much slippery as sticky. Never mind dangerous; this is the kind of stuff you can really let go on. You just whack your feet in and it yields like soft mud, making it twice as fast as a solid path and half as painful. I lengthen my stride and, for the first time in miles, run for the fun of it.

By the time I regain control at the point where the path leaves the scree halfway down, I've overtaken the pair in front of me and drawn level with another group: two stringy men and a steaming, red-faced woman. And I'm just in time for another surprise: in a split second, the clouds disappear utterly. Instantly, all around, the view is so dazzlingly clear that it is impossible to imagine it ever having been overcast. A monumental rim of mountains juts up around us, into a gleaming sky. To our left, Kirk Fell and Great Gable shimmer like mighty castles, every detail carved as sharp as flint; somewhere below, the fresh water of Lingmell Beck sparkles dazzlingly; straight ahead, brilliantly coloured miniature people scuttle across the grass at Sty Head, mysterious as tiny details in an old painting; and, beyond them, who knows what hills and valleys stretch off up to Scotland as they have done for millennia.

The scale of it, the sheer miraculous clarity of it, is so shocking that the trio in front slow to a half-walk, as do I.

"Bloody hell," says the hindmost, to his companions and to me. "That's what we do it for, eh?" We all grunt our agreement; and then, gradually, pick up speed again, re-focussing on the stones beneath our feet. That is, I suppose, what we do it for. All those hours – days – of cloud cold and misery and sore feet: they're the price that runners, like walkers, pay for a few glorious moments when the clouds part and everything snaps into focus like a slide. That's what country pursuits are all about. Or is it?

Over the next few hours, as my muscles stiffen and my bruises deepen and the clear brilliance turns to torturing heat, I try to distract myself by pondering this point; and, the more I do so, the more I have my doubts. The great Bob Graham, originator of and for three decades the only man to complete the Bob Graham Round (42 of the Lake District's highest peaks in 24 hours), was suspicious of views. Spend a minute on each peak enjoying the view, he once remarked, and you've added 42 minutes to your time. That's a rather joyless way of looking at it; but then so too, I would argue, is the conventional way of looking at it, in which the only real purpose of the countryside is to enjoy the view. Just a few days before the race, the papers had been full of reports of a survey in which readers of *Country Life* magazine chose Britain's best views: Salisbury Cathedral, Buttermere, Three Cliffs Bay: the usual suspects, all described in terms of the same virtues – tranquillity, serenity, timelessness – with photographs to match. Was it just me, or was there something about the exercise that sapped the will to live?

Sometimes I think you can tell a person's age by their attitude to views. As a child, there's nothing duller than to be told "Look at the view." Yes, never mind that, what are we going to *do?* Then you begin to spend long stretches of your life imprisoned in offices, traffic jams and shops; visions of rural splendour begin to seem more precious. By middle age, it has become second nature to look, not at where you are, but at the furthest available horizon. Perhaps decades of habitual disappointment have stripped immediate reality of its charms, whereas the distance retains the magic of infinite possibility. Eventually you become so immobile that the countryside becomes one enormous view, to be looked at, ideally, from the comfort of a tea-shop. And good luck to all of them, say I; or, rather, I would if I didn't keep thinking that, in the way we discuss the countryside these days – with our constant emphasis on tranquillity and tradition – we sometimes seem to be embracing the perspective of the elderly to the exclusion of all else. This is what bothers me about the cult of the view: nothing wrong with it per se; but I fear that it is blinding a lot of people to the real riches of our rural heritage.

The best English view I ever saw was, I think, of Headcorn, Kent. Headcorn is one of those Home Counties villages so cocooned in civilised comforts that they're all but suburban. But the great advantage of this view was that I was looking at it from 11,000ft up, on my first and last skydive. The patchwork of green fields and orchards spread unimaginably far, curving at the edge of my vision with the planet. Cars and shops were invisible; villages were brown smudges around ancient churches; wherever I focused, there was mystery, pattern, fecundity – and an intoxicating sense that all was, despite everything, rather well with rural England. I was almost persuaded to go back for another jump.

My next best view was probably another fell-running

moment, coming off the back of Skiddaw in the middle of a midsummer night and watching shooting stars falling like golden petals over Great Calva and Blencathra; or, alternatively, a few hours later on the same run, watching the sun come up below us as we ran along the Helvellyn ridge, with the whole Lake District sleeping for miles on either side under a soft blanket of grass and mist. And then there were all those other views – countless moments, all, I'm afraid, sounding equally macho: a line of bloodhounds streaking across a frosty hillside at dawn, hot on my scent, as I crouch in a puddle waiting for them; a wide, bleak stretch of rocky Northumberland coast, seen, as the Vikings first saw it, from low down in an icy sea; or the tranquil, sweet-scented Welsh valley – complete with tangled hedges, sleepy village and wild-flower meadow – in which I found myself, half-dead with fright, when my first and last experience of flat-out downhill mountain-biking finally came to a merciful halt.

All very hearty, you might think. But that's not my point. Oscar Wilde, who knew little of heartiness or of rural life, put it rather better when he wrote: "It seems to me that we all look at Nature too much, and live with her too little. I discern great sanity in the Greek attitude. They never chattered about sunsets, or discussed whether the shadows on the lawn were really mauve or not. But they saw that the sea was for the swimmer, and the sand for the feet of the runner. They loved the trees for the shadow that they cast, and the forest for its silence at noon..." Anyone who hunts, or shoots, or fishes, or farms, will know what Wilde meant. It's a fancy way of saying that, if you're not cold, or wet, or lost, or exhausted, or torn by brambles or covered in mud, you're not really experiencing the countryside properly. The point is not the exertion involved: it's the degree of involvement, or immersion, in the landscape. You need to *feel* it, to interact with it; to be *in* it, not just looking from the outside. But, of course, the number of people who hunt and farm and so forth is dwindling daily; and, as it does so, the tyranny of the view is spreading. It would be a pity if it did so unchallenged.

New breeds of countryside-lover are inheriting the land: day-trippers, commuters, telecommuters, migrants from towns. 'Real' country folk traditionally sneer at such people; but the outsiders now outnumber the insiders, and it is in their hands that the future of the countryside lies. Most of them are as gentle and anxious to avoid giving offence as any other English people; and so they approach the countryside in what they believe to be the approved way, congregating as directed at viewpoints and picnic areas to gaze obediently at scenic England as if it were an art gallery, speaking in hushed voices and keeping off the grass. No wonder they don't understand the countryside. Yet most Britons aren't naturally like that. Most Britons are under 45. Most have never known a world without roaring traffic, urban sprawl, cacophonous mass media and music; for all but a handful, normality is a crowded street, a bustling city, a blaring television, a busy, hectic round of getting, spending and rapid gratification. That doesn't make them immune to the less frantic charms of the English countryside; or, for that matter, to the richness of the past. It does make them less likely to engage with a rural heritage that is presented to them exclusively through an elderly, backward-looking filter.

Like it or not, there are millions of people in Britain – all potential guardians of the countryside – who, through no fault of their own, are not yet middle-aged. They don't want to be sedate. The question is: is there a place for them in the countryside or not? In fact, thousands of them are claiming such a place, whether we want them to or not. Hence the boom – often deplored – in a whole host of country sports that had never been dreamt of in the days before the motor car. Not fell-running (which had), but mountain-biking, trail-biking, hang-gliding, wind-surfing, adventure-racing and so on; none of which would normally be looked on as a 'country sport' and none of which involves gazing tranquilly at views; but all of which involve – no less than fox-hunting – getting out in the countryside, becoming (in one way or another) intimate with the landscape, and emerging happier – and probably better – as a result.

Should we welcome these rude incomers – tens of thousands of them – and admit that they too are countrymen and -women? Or should we retreat to the clichés of the brochures and the magazines, in which the meaning of the phrase 'the English countryside' has been narrowed to encompass only those parts of our rural heritage that are rooted in the past: vanishing flora and fauna, quiet lanes and historic churches, quaint cottages and sleepy village greens? Is our ideal rural scene *unspoilt* – redolent less of 2002 than of 1902? Or is it somewhere where we may legitimately seek thrills, action, challenge? I know which I prefer. I believe that the countryside is not for looking at but for doing things in. Of course, there are virtues in tranquillity. But to claim it as the prime rural virtue is to risk comparison with the old lady in the public swimming-pool who tuts and curses every time a passer-by is thoughtless enough to splash. To engage truly with the

English countryside in one's leisure hours is not just to escape the sound and fury of the urban treadmill; it is also a matter (and this thought occurred to me in the fifth hour of my race, on the steep, tussocky, bouldery, agonising descent from Dale Head) of casting off the formalities of civilisation. That is what country sports, ancient and modern, have in common. They are not so much leisure pursuits as rituals; less to do with the pursuit of happiness than with the discovery of self, or reconnection with the inner animal. They are, in short, about satisfying the old human thirst for adventure. Whether or not they bring you in contact with beautiful sights is beside the point.

Sometimes, though, they do – which brings me back to Borrowdale, and, specifically, to another of my favourite views. It is the same day and the same race, except that, blissfully, the race is over. There's nowhere to shower or change (this is fell-running, remember), and nothing to drink but the shared contents of a dustbin of saliva-flecked orange squash. Yet somehow or other I need to make myself feel human again. So I hobble down the lane to a stony track which leads in turn to a little knee-deep ford behind a field, crossed by stepping stones and hung about with old green trees. And here, for fully 15 minutes, I lie down in the cool stream. Never have I felt such comfort: the smooth stones beneath, the gentle massaging of the current, the feel and scent and taste of the sweetest fresh water. But the view, too, seems supernaturally perfect: dappled, liquid shadows in the foreground, and, visible through a gap in the leaves, a line of green mountains shining beneath a clear blue sky.

I am looking at England at its best. More importantly, I am immersed in it.

[36]

DAVID BELLAMY & PIERS BROWNE

The glorious trees of Great Britain

For the past 15 years, the artist Piers Browne has been travelling his native land, creating a pictorial record of his great passion: trees. The result: a stunning collection of nearly 300 oil paintings and etchings, which he is now revealing to the world in the form of an exhibition and a book, both in aid of the Conservation Foundation. Over the following pages, we present a selection of Browne's etchings, while David Bellamy, who has written much of the text for the book, introduces Browne's work and writes expert pen-portraits of his subjects

FOUR SCORE YEARS AND TEN ARE BUT A TWINKLING IN THE time scale of life upon this Earth, while 3.6 billion is just too long for us even to contemplate. Perhaps that is why we, mere mortals, have so long stood in reverence of trees, each one a pillar of knowledge stretching up to the cathedral of the skies while casting its cooling *ombrage* of wisdom over the panoply of life. Today the clever men of science can read the story of their lives writ small in every trunk and every wetland that stores carbon as wood or peat. Each tree trunk is made of millions of long, thin, woody elements. These once living cells gave their lives in the call of duty, their lot not only to carry life-giving water from roots to leaves but to store megabytes of environmental information laid down in their rings of growth, season by season, year by year. Viewed beneath a microscope, the width and luxuriance of these elements of truth tell how good each season was at producing the cells that gave life to the tree and strength and lasting beauty to its wood.

Each trunk, whether still growing, or preserved in a medieval building, a prehistoric burial mound or a peat swamp, is a time-capsule of intricate information concerning our ever-changing climate. As it grows in girth, being weather-wise, it is a self-recording barometer of the past and is the litmus of environmental change. Collate all the information stored on these hard discs together and you have an age-old database detailing the vagaries of the global greenhouse, at least over the timescale of what I would like to call the Time Lord Trees.

Piers Browne's pictures, shown on the following pages, are one man's interpretation of the wisdom of the Time Lords here in Britain, crafted at a time when destruction of their ancient world has reached a suicidal rate.

OAK

Piers Browne was a Shropshire lad brought up in a house partly made of recycled naval ships of the Hearts of Oak armada line. It stands upright to this day, still held together with wooden plugs. Little wonder then that you will find the soul of Britain in his pictures, for this is a man who can see both the wood and the trees in all their glory.

Pollard oaks: Knebworth

Our native oaks returned to Britain after the last Ice Age some 10,000 years ago. They added their own substance to the shattered landscape as they helped make and hold the rich soils of England, Scotland and Wales. Our ancestors evolved within the kingdom whose landscapes were ruled by oaks. Shade they cast in plenty, but the effect of their presence was more all-embracing: the atmosphere itself became heavy with an effleurage of the special chemicals that, distilled from the summer canopy of leaves and the rich mulch of winter litter, gave Britain's unique natural background a homeopathy of healing chemicals which some believe help regulate our own internal chemistry and hence our lives. It is a remedy which changes with the seasons.

The sleep of winter lets the fungi of damp decay reign supreme, recycling everything that is needed for another year. Spring's birth unfolds all buds that shine with protective resins as flowers come into bloom and leaves unfold. Summer matures and insects do their worst, leaving the leaves in tatters despite the protective chemicals they produce. In August comes the oaks' special season of Lammastide, when each tree produces a new crop of soft, luscious leaves to feed the insect larvae ready for their winter sleep, and thus heralds autumn when the goodness in the green of chlorophyll is recycled to reveal the many splendoured tints of autumn – then back to the well-earned rest of winter.

ASH

In the North, the place of the oak is taken by the ash. It grows fast and can outlive the oak. Its divided, compound leaves cast but a light shadow and so allow a diverse flora to grow on the rich mulch soils they help to create. Ash glades

Weeping ash: sleet in December

attract the game to feed. Well-lit, they are places of easy quarry, fast food for those whose only source of sustenance was to hunt and gather the richness of the forests. The same was of course true for the trees themselves, for their soft leaves are the first to be drawn underground by worms, and so the goodness they contain is rapidly turned to humus that holds the minerals safe, ready to charge the sap as it rises in the spring of another year. It was the favourite timber for fuelling fires, as it will burn well while still green.

In Norse mythology the ash is 'yggdrasill', the Great World Tree and the strong axis around which the three planes of existence revolve and in whose roots dwells the serpent of infinite libido. A goat, which fed on the leaves, gave milk to the heroes of Valhalla, and at the moment of destruction of the world this tree became a guardian mother regenerating a whole new race of people. The Vikings built their boats and made the shafts of their spears from its strong wood. Mothers hung their cradles from its branches seeking protection for their babies from evil spirits. Its use in medicine and magic are legion: on Christmas Eve the burning of an ashen faggot was a popular fire charm ceremony in inns and farmhouses, helping maidens to find their swains when nothing was luckier than, an 'even as', an even number of these pinnate leaves – 13 being our common or European ash's norm prior to any conflagration.

BEECH

Of all our deciduous Time Lords, beech casts the deepest shade, so deep that little or nothing can grow beneath its canopy. Native only in south England and Wales, it has been planted across the length and breadth of Britain both as a windbreak and for the utility of its wood. When the Romans arrived in Britain much of our wild wood had already been destroyed. Without the presence of the Time Lord trees our high rainfall had washed away the rich forest soils, turning their mull to moor, their good earth to the grey earth called podsols, common to carboniferous floor covering and in places so acid that only heath, moor and bog could thrive. The peatlands, spreading across mountains and lowlands alike, took down the evidence preserving great tree trunks and the pollen grains those trees and other plants had in vain scattered on the wind.

Beech wood lasts well in waterlogged soils: millers used it for their sluices and wheels; parts of Winchester Cathedral, built around 35 years before the Norman

Copper beech in high gale

Conquest, still stand on beech piles – as did old Waterloo Bridge. The leaves of the beech are tougher than those of the ash and so hold their store of energy and minerals longer, releasing them to feed a whole foray of fungi that pass the minerals on to succour the Time Lords. Peasant people came to know that they could feed on the fungi, but if bad times forced them to collect too many of the leaves from the forest floor to use as litter for their animals, then catastrophe in the form of acid soils was not far away.

ELM
Despite the fact that it is the Christian symbol for strength, the mighty elm showed its weakness to attack by a deadly fungus which wiped millions of these trees off the face of John Constable's Britain – and sadly continues its work. The elms had arrived in force at about the same time as

Camperdown elm: sunrise

the oaks, long before the seas had risen to fill up the English Channel and thus to block further incursions.

The pollen runes tell the story in great detail with elms reaching high into the sky from Willy Lots's Suffolk cottage in the south to the top of Cross Fell in the Pennines, and beyond. North, south, east and west, this was their demesne, but their nutrient rich leaves, which fed a host of insects, were to be their undoing. The first cowboys turned up on the sylvan scene bringing tame aurochs with them and at first stripped the leaves from off the elms to feed these cattle. Then, with axes of polished stone made in the

Langdale factories, they set about removing the trees to make way for the landscape the poet came to know so well. This process of change, helped by the warmer, wetter, global greenhouse and exacerbated by the burning of the ancient forests, from that time on led to the rapid disappearance of the wild wood. The Time Lord Trees were relegated to serfdom and allowed to grow only in forgotten places or where they were told. Their trunks burned where they lay and poured carbon dioxide into the heavy air.

CHESTNUTS

Chestnuts are not native but have found a special place in both formal and informal landscapes and hence in the hearts of people. Knowing of its utility both as a staple food and for making the handles for tools, as poles for hops and vines and staves for the cooper's art, the Romans introduced sweet chestnut into Britain. It became the most coppiceable of all our trees. When the first Neolithic axe-man stood back to survey his fell deed, little did he know of the full power of this Time Lord's hidden magic. With the controlling influence of the leading shoot gone, buds latent around the butt began to sprout; they formed a ring of strong young shoots fertilised by the ash of the burnt waste wood. This juvenile wood was a constant supply that could be put to many different uses. Most of the new shoots were felled after a period of between 12 and 20 years to be used to fuel the hearth or as handles for an ever-increasing variety of tools. The strongest were singled out and left to grow to maturity, their ultimate fate to become structural components for timbered buildings and the bulk of sailing ships of many lines.

So it was that parts of our countryside underwent a sylvan renaissance in which the Time Lords became stewards

Flowering chestnut: Wales from near Hereford

in a new bio-diverse and beautiful woodland called 'coppice with standards'. Each stage in their cycle of management provided a home for flowers and the insects, birds and mammals that depended upon them. The horse chestnut, with its summer candles of white flowers, was much later introduced from Greece, probably as an ornamental tree, although, since time immemorial, every herbal bath worth a soaking has contained the bitter essence of the conker.

Piers Browne's The Glorious Trees of Great Britain, *with introductions by the Prince of Wales and David Bellamy, is published by The Shorthorn Press (£35), in aid of the Conservation Foundation. An exhibition of the pictures is at The North Light Gallery, Huddersfield, until 14 December (tel: 01484 340003 for details).*

NEAL ASCHERSON

Death of a village

IN THE SUMMER OF 1848, MORE THAN 40 PEOPLE WERE
living at Arichonan in North Knapdale. The ruins of their
homes and byres are still there, on a high terrace of land
several hundred feet above sea level. There is a long view to
the south over the fjords of Caol Scotnish and Loch Sween.
A burn of clean water runs out of the hill and past the
houses. In front of the settlement, the level spaces overgrown with bracken and brambles were once strip-fields
under oats and potatoes. About 10 houses and outbuild-
ings can still be made out. A tweed-dyeing boiler lies
among the nettles and a broken iron cauldron nearly 4ft
across. The last farmer, who lived on his own among the
ruins and built chimneys and gables onto his own house
out of the fallen stones around him, left a metal bedstead,
now lying on the grass in front of his hearthstone.

Arichonan in 1848 was a 'multiple tenancy', the
ancient settlement pattern in which a group of family
heads jointly shared the land. The soil was poor and often

[47]

uneven in its fertility; to prevent unfairness, the people would usually hold an annual ballot to decide which family would have the use of each strip ('rig') of arable. Each summer Arichonan's small black cattle would be driven to the hilltop pastures above, joining the beasts from other settlements nearby and watched over by children and young people camping out in the temporary shelters and cabins known as 'shielings'

Too much is made of the 'organic' difference between Highland and Lowland Scotland. Most of the difference is relatively recent: the result of a divergence between the two regions which began in the Middle Ages. Anyone who goes looking for some equivalent of a clan system in the medieval Lowlands will find plenty of evidence. Basic social arrangements were pretty similar in territories supposedly 'Celtic' or 'Teutonic'. Allowing for worse weather, worse soil and the Gaelic language culture, the Arichonan type of community (baile, in Gaelic) strongly resembled the Lowland 'ferm touns' that were swept away in the late 18th century. What the ruins do not resemble is a modern crofting township, with its widely separated houses. Instead, Arichonan was a tight, cosy maze of stone walls and buildings, narrow paved closes once overhung by heather-thatched eaves, tiny yards and bothies, secret corners and hiding places. It must have been a good place for small children. On a cornerstone in one of the ruins, a man carved his name: 'Niel Macmillan'. Two things are known about him: that he was the father of 10 children, who lived with their parents at Arichonan until 1848; and that he was evidently literate. A man who could write, even though he was shaky at the spelling of his own name, would have been able to read. But what did he read, and is

[48]

it possible that newspapers reached Arichonan during the early months of that fiery year?

The papers carried news of revolution, beginning at Palermo in January and spreading to France in February. Monarchies fell and liberal constitutions were granted. By March, the revolution had gripped the German states and Austria; Hungary rose and so did smaller Slav nationalities who feared Hungary as much as they feared the Hapsburgs. In the United Kingdom, the 'Young Ireland' movement threatened armed insurrection and a programme of land reform, while that April the Chartists held their climactic, gigantic, futile rally for political reform in London. All over Britain, landowners cleaned their fowling-pieces and nervously watched the night horizon for the flames of arson.

From the hill above Arichonan, on a very clear day, you can just see the shadow of Ireland. Elizabeth Grant of Rothiemurchus, the 'Highland Lady' whose memoirs and diaries are a unique personal record of her times, had begun life as a young girl in Edinburgh and Speyside. Now, in 1848, she had become an expatriate Irish landowner, married to Colonel Henry Smith and managing the big house and estate of Baltiboys, near Dublin. Like many intelligent property-owners in times of political upheaval, she was at first excited by the overthrow of dilapidated regimes. "This news (of the revolution in France) must have some effect in England, where we are very nearly ready for a similar revolution. The higher classes cannot much longer be allowed to live in idleness principally from the proceeds of the labour of the middle ranks, enjoying peculiar privileges unearned by any merit," she wrote in her diary in March. "They had quite a right to depose their

King if he did not govern them satisfactorily, and if tired of monarchs, as we all shall be bye and bye, they choose to try a republick, it is nobody's business to question their wisdom." But by the end of April 1848, she was anxious. 'The mob', especially in Ireland, was denouncing landed property itself, not just the privileges which it conferred. Riots spread through English and Scottish cities, and there were hopeless armed risings in the Irish countryside. She still thought that aristocracy should surrender its privileges, but "the property and the greater part of the intelligence of the country are against any description of tumult."

All around her, Ireland was perishing and emigrating in the fifth year of the Great Famine. Daughter of a chiefly family in the northern Highlands, Elizabeth Grant had been raised to believe in duthchas, the mutual relationship which linked the chief's duty of protection to the personal loyalty and obedience of his people. The Famine faced her with an utterly different relationship which she was never able to accept: human suffering on a scale far beyond the means of even a benevolent landowner to relieve, and tenants who felt no traditional duty to masters whom in their hearts they regarded as alien oppressors. In Argyll, elements of duthchas still survived – among the common people, if no longer among the chiefs and the profit-orientated landowners who were rapidly replacing them. But famine was there too. In Ireland, the potato blight had struck in 1845. It arrived in Scotland a year later. Famine was mainly confined to the Highlands and Islands, where the potato had become the mainstay diet of families driven or resettled from their traditional lands to make way for sheep. It was never as severe as in Ireland. There was no mass starvation, and – as Tom Devine explains in his book

[51]

Clanship to Crofters' War – there were job opportunities in the Scottish industrial cities, while the provision of relief by landowners was incomparably better organised than in Ireland. Above all, most of Scotland south and east of the Highlands was relatively unaffected. This encouraged a powerful philanthropic relief effort by the rest of the country. But the impact of the blight on the fragile subsistence economy of the Highlands and Islands was none the less disastrous. While there was no dying on the Irish scale, the death rate rose steeply, assisted – as in Ireland – by typhus and other famine-related diseases. Relief was efficient, but offered by the Central Board of Management for Highland Relief on heartless and humiliating terms. Those who passed the 1848 Destitution Test received a pound of oatmeal for a day's labour; half a pound was offered to the old and infirm, while children were to be fed only on evidence that their school attendance was regular.

Sir Charles Trevelyan, assistant secretary to the Treasury, oversaw relief in Scotland on the free-market principles he had applied to such lethal effect in Ireland. In a letter to the Celtic historian William Skene, a member of the Central Board, Trevelyan wrote that "the pound of meal and the task of at least eight hours' and work is the best regime for this moral disease." But, desperate as their situation was by 1848, four out of five people in Wester Ross and three-quarters of the people of Skye looked to their honour and refused to take the Destitution Test. The most obvious result of the famine was that emigration from the Highlands and Islands reached levels never seen before or since. Many thousands left for Canada and Australia between 1846 and 1857; unknown thousands more chose 'internal emigration' and arrived on the rainy pavements of Scottish cities. Some of this movement was voluntary, with 'assisted' passages wholly or partly paid for by the landlords. Some of it was coerced 'clearance'. As relief payments wound down and the famine receded, landowners feared that support for the destitute would now fall on their own shoulders; the rural poor had to be removed before they became a liability. The methods used combined carrot and stick in many different proportions. They ranged from benevolent offers of free passage to Canada to the use of clubs and the firing of thatch to evict households unable or unwilling to pay increased rents.

Alan Begg, a local historian at Kilmartin in Mid-Argyll, writes: "The infamous Highland Clearances ... didn't happen much in this part of Scotland, as the lairds used other ways to get their hands on the land... the lairds forced the rents up and up until eventually the crofters had to give up. The other method was not to renew leases, which was a regular practice." In Argyll, the outcome of either method was much the same. The emptied landscape would be turned over to blackface 'Linton' sheep, the joint-tenancy bailtean would be replaced by a single tenant farmer in a slate-roofed house with chimneys, and bracken would grow over the pastures once kept green by cattle. In the decade after 1846, the population of many parishes and even whole islands fell by between a third and a half. The parish of North Knapdale around Arichonan held 2,170 persons in 1841. By 1851, in the third year of famine, the population had fallen by about a quarter, to 1,666. By 1881, it numbered only 927.

Mid-Argyll had experienced the dissolution of the clan system and the development of a cash economy much earlier than the northern and western Highlands. North

Knapdale, including Arichonan, had been bought by a speculating businessman in the 1790s, who sold it to the Malcolms in 1801. By then, the Malcolms had already accumulated great wealth; in the late 18th century their Jamaica estates and business were returning the huge sum of £40,000 a year, and they began to purchase territory in South Australia in 1839. They possessed estates and country houses in England and bought a succession of large town houses in London. In their new Argyll properties, they poured capital and energy into a development programme which transformed the landscape and the life of its inhabitants over the next 50 years; they invested in the construction of the Crinan Canal, began the systematic draining of the Crinan Moss bog with trenches 11ft deep, peeled the accumulated peat off the alluvial soils of Kilmartin Glen and replaced traditional cottages with solid houses of stone and slate.

They were efficient, paternalistic landlords. Unlike some of the worst proprietors in the north and the isles, the Malcolms tried to avoid the use of force and showed concern for the fate of their tenantry; Neill Malcolm III not only paid for passages to Canada and Australia but apparently provided ongoing grants to support Poltalloch tenants while they found their feet in Ontario. None the less, the remnants of the old baile joint-tenancies, with their non-commercial subsistence agriculture and their inability to pay viable rents, stood in their way. Until the land could be worked by larger commercial farms, with the hills cleared for sheep, the estates stood no chance of returning a profit. The joint-tenancies had to go, and their inhabitants with them. The famine made the change seem even more urgent. The method which the Malcolms appear to have preferred was to increase rents on the tenancies and then to serve eviction notices for non-payment. There is no record of resistance or 'any description of tumult' before 1848. But at Arichonan, something went wrong. The rents were raised, and the people refused to pay. Eviction notices were twice served, and the people refused to leave. This was unusual. Something new was in the air in that rebellious year, not just in the hills but throughout the district.

Neill Malcolm was away, and in his absence the estate factor (manager) and the authorities panicked. A posse of nine policemen, with the Poltalloch factor, the Sheriff Officer and 25 estate workers, climbed up the track to Arichonan to serve the final eviction notice. One version of what happened tells that the men of Arichonan had been drawn away from the houses by a ruse, and that the raiding party found themselves faced by a rank of defiant women. What is certain is that the posse met resistance. A large crowd, which soon grew to over 300 as people ran up from nearby settlements, confronted them. The police seized a few men as hostages and the posse retreated downhill to Bellanoch on the Crinan Canal, pursued by the crowd which besieged them in the Bellanoch inn.

Two local men who had the people's trust, the innkeeper at Crinan and the well-respected farmer at Ardifuar, George Campbell, were brought in to mediate. The prisoners were released, and the arrest party made its way back to the small town of Lochgilphead, only to find the streets full of people roaring their support for the families of Arichonan. The Sheriff wrote to Edinburgh demanding the despatch of troops "by the quick steamer". In Ireland, the troops would have been sent and blood would have been shed. But the Edinburgh authorities, their own resources stretched by rioting and Chartist demonstrations, decided that Mid-Argyll could clear up its own mess. To borrow one of Elizabeth Grant's favourite sayings, Argyll could "give its ain fish guts to its ain sea mews". They sent no soldiers. In the long run, the men and women of Arichonan could not win. They surrendered, but may have won some assurance of lenient treatment. As Michael Davis records in his study *Poltalloch and the Transformation of Mid-Argyll*, they were later persuaded to leave Arichonan "after negotiations in Gaelic... only five individuals were sentenced, and these lightly by the standards of the day (eight months in Inveraray Jail)". What happened to them afterwards is unknown. Sheep were moved on to their abandoned lands, and one cottage was rebuilt to house a shepherd.

The Irish Famine was by far the greatest human catastrophe in 19th-century Europe. Between 1845 and 1850, around a million people died of hunger or of disease associated with hunger (some historians put it higher, but there will never be precise figures). The death toll and the pell-mell emigration which followed reduced the population of Ireland from over eight million to 6.5 million in only 10 years. The whole course of social and economic development in southern Ireland was irrevocably changed. The famine's legacy of grief and anger to Ireland and to the post-famine diaspora, above all in North America, still shapes Irish political instincts in the 21st century. The Highland Clearances were a lesser, slower tragedy. But as memory and myth they still provide a powerful component of Scottish political instincts, and not only in the Highlands. Just as Irish-Americans have sought to have the Famine accepted as part of the 'Holocaust Studies' curriculum at American universities, so a number of Scottish scholars and writers seek to understand the Clearances as a form of genocide, cultural rather than physical, which deliberately destroyed Gaelic society through a prolonged act of 'ethnic cleansing'. In both cases, the motive is patriotic. These are attempts to hitch national experience on to universal bandwagons: most recently, to the victimologies of the 20th century from Auschwitz to Bosnia. Several previous efforts were made to reinvent the Clearances in this way. The first began while the Clearances were still in progress, when they were represented by Victorian radicals as the inevitable consequence of aristocratic landlordism and privilege, an evil anachronism which was under attack by liberals and land reformers all over Europe. The second reinvention – and the most persuasive – arrived in the 20th century. Socialists identified the cause of the Clearances as the impact of the cash economy and market forces on a traditional, collectivist society; clan chiefs used their authority to become aggressive capitalists for whom people and land became exchangeable commodities.

Today, as a mild Land Reform programme is put through the Scottish Parliament, all three versions are in vigorous use – sometimes in the same speech. The Highland Clearance myth, employed as a sort of victim's ticket to board the world, remains an integral part of Scottish identity. A 'myth' is not necessarily untrue. It means, as I use the term, a historical narrative which is used to support wider assumptions about moral worth or national identity. The Clearances happened, and they were a human disaster – at times, an atrocity – on a grand scale. One of Europe's small peoples, rich in its oral culture and its ingenious forms of community, was uprooted, pauperised, not infrequently terrorised and driven out of its own country. Living landscapes became dead, soggy wildernesses. A beautiful language was treated as a shameful patois and pushed to the edge of extinction.

Quantifying the Clearances is difficult and also misleading. The population of Scotland by 1841 was about 2.6 million, of which the Highlands and Islands accounted for less than 250,000. At the height of the Clearances, in the decade after 1847, some 16,000 people emigrated from the Highlands to North America and Australia. The net Highland population loss between 1855 and 1895 was only about nine per cent – not much more than the decline in many parts of the Lowlands. But this conceals the difference between displacement and depopulation. Most of those evicted or rack-rented out of their homes did not board the emigrant ships but were resettled within the Highlands – generally on barren strips of coastline where the only reliable crop was potatoes. In many cases, and above all after the famine, their lives were materially worse than those of the emigrants who had gone weeping to the boats but had found fertile soil allotted to them in Ontario or South Australia. Equally important, those who had been removed to the coast were still the helpless tenants of landlords against whom they had no legal protection whatever. But the emigrants, clearing virgin forest off a Canadian homestead deep in snow, had the consolation of knowing that at last they owned the land they lived on. No laird, no rent-collector, no factor with an eviction order would ever trouble them or their children again.

Extracted from Stone Voices: The Search for Scotland, *by Neal Ascherson (Granta, £16.99)*

JONATHAN ROBERTS

A hill farmer's year

I AM VERY LUCKY. I LIVE AND WORK ON A HILL SHEEP-farm in West Dorset. I inhabit a secret world with only one entrance or exit: a long, gloomy, overgrown rabbit-hole of a lane whose steep sides are revetted by ivy and ferns. In spring the lane is a sunken garden of wild prim-roses, violets and celandines. In summer it becomes a dark tunnel, overarched by branches of hazel, holly and ash. A friend wearing sunglasses once drove up it on a bright summer's day and crashed into the side because every-thing went black. When you climb out of the rabbit-hole on to my hill, you are confronted by perhaps one of the most beautiful views in southern England, across the coombs and goyles that undulate down towards Bridport, Golden Cap and Lyme Regis. Away to the left is Eggardon Hill. In the distance you can see the sea.

The Romans arrived here shortly after the Claudian invasion in 44AD and built a fort on top of the hill behind my house; a biggish fort, if barrack foundations are anything to go by (the site was excavated in the 1960s), housing many men. I like to think the view reminded the Romans of some hilltop hamlet in Umbria. In those days they would have looked out over an unbroken wildwood rug of trees, rather like the Apennines back home, with the odd clearing for cultivation. The native population of our entire island was then perhaps a million at most, and land-use for agriculture was more or less non-existent. The wildwood in West Dorset was first colonised into fields and farms in Saxon times, and the view has remained just about the same ever since. It is a highly artificial, man-made construct of grass and arable enclosures, neat hedges, tidy farms, quiet hamlets, churches with square-topped towers, hanging woods of beech, ash and oak. In the far distance, looking like oil rigs on the rim of the sea, you can just make out the line of electricity pylons that march across the Marshwood vale and up the side of Eggardon. It is a view that has evolved – and refreshed and sustained, I think, many weary souls – for more than 1,000 years. I am proud to share it with the walkers using the footpath that traverses the spine of my farm. It is a view that, morning and evening, summer and winter, I never tire of admiring. And it is a view for whose future, over the next 50 years, I am fearful.

If and when the farmers go, and the cattle and sheep disappear, will the fields revert back to the wildwood that the Romans saw? Will brambles, ragwort, bracken and gorse inherit the land? Will the churches that I can see in the middle distance become deconsecrated for holiday units, the farmhouses sold for second homes? Will the hamlets become housing estates? Will West Dorset become a metropolitan suburb? Such are the gloomy reflections (written on the eve of the 2002 harvest festival – that metaphorical red line under the farmer's year) of a hill sheep-farmer in West Dorset. Official statistics are not encouraging. They tell me that I am rushing to leave the industry, that the national sheep-stock is shrinking fast, that the price of wool does not cover the cost of shearing, that my average age is 58 (actually, I am 59), that nobody wants English lamb, that my income is less than the minimum wage, that I am deep in debt to the bank, that I must diversify or die, that I am on tranquillisers, that my back is gone, that I shake like a leaf from sheep-dip, that I am as likely as a vet or a dentist to shoot myself in a rather messy way among the cabbages of the vegetable garden. And so on, and so on.

Some of this – in my case bad back, shrinking flock, trying to diversify – I freely admit to. I have cut down to zero the commercial, indoor-lambing flock of Mules that I used to keep. Now I run a few old Swaledale ewes that lamb themselves down, with a minimum of fuss, out on the rough hill. They are squat, hardy sheep with black faces, mean eyes, coarse wool, thick, forward-curving horns, and cantankerous natures. Since the Men from the Ministry purged their Yorkshire Dales during last year's foot-and-mouth epidemic, there are not many of them left. They scare the daylights out of any foxes or badgers (of which there are too many in these parts) that get between them and their lambs. During the lambing season, my border collie, Tommy, has to watch out for himself not to get a crack in the ribs from some indignant ewe.

No self-respecting, low-ground shepherd would entertain such sheep nowadays – they have an irritating habit of getting their horns stuck in the gates of handling-races.

But I have a soft spot for my Swaleys. They make the most of the sunshine when it is available, and endure the wind, cold and rain with equanimity. They are loyal mums, their feet are durable and they suffer less from *Fusiformis nodosus* – aka foot-rot, that stinking, horrible bane of sheep and shepherds – than most other breeds. Poor grazing suits them. They get put to a Texel ram in October, and by the end of March, when the daffodils and yellow primroses are in bloom and the ravens are croaking in the Monterey pines that overshadow my lane, the lambing-field is full of chunky, fluffy white lambs playing race-you-away-from-the-tree or I'm-the-king-of-the-castle. They do not make me much money, my Swaleys, but I love to see them spread out with their lambs higgledy-piggledy across a hillside like bulbs chucked from a bucket. Providing the fencing is good enough to hold them, they will graze a field down as close as any lawnmower, and they are partial to noxious weeds like docks and Oxford ragwort. Only nettles, foxgloves, bracken and thistles are rejected (I have to deal with these by laborious use of a knapsack sprayer on the steepest slopes), and they will even chew old nettles late in the season when the bite of the stings has diminished. Sheep are wonderful animals for creating and maintaining grass landscape – no landscape gardener should be without them – and if you have decent fences and the ability to move stock from field to field, their golden hoof will give you a cricket-pitch sward. The old saying, "Sheep should never hear church bells twice in the same field", still obtains.

I am a dog-and-stick farmer, or very nearly so. When my wife and I moved down from Scotland 10 years ago, and bought our Dorset farm, she looked at the slopes involved and said yes, she'd move, but I'd have to run the farm without the assistance of a tractor. She was right, of course: I would have killed myself on the slopes long ago. I make do with a quad bike, which is like an extra sheep-dog, but I still like to look at the sheep on foot and use my ears, in exquisite engine-free silence, for noise of sheep caught in brambles or on the wrong side of a fence. Anyway, as I get older, I like to walk. I get a chance to see the green woodpeckers – they call them yaffles in this part of the world – feeding on the yellow anthills on the sunny side of the hill, and there is usually a roe deer out grazing in the evening, and a buzzard or two soaring overhead. Sometimes the ravens in the Monterey pines take on the buzzards, and there is an aerial battle-royal, with much croaking and complaint. The ravens always win.

And diversification? I let out most of the better acres now to other graziers, and the rough, steep hill where I run my sheep I have put into a Countryside Stewardship scheme, which pays me money to cut-and-lay the hazel hedges in the winter and not to use fertiliser or sprays. A local agent explained to me that the old landlord-tenant system has been turned upside down in recent years. In the old days, in this area, there were one or two large land-lords and many small tenants. Now, farms are being bought up by city men who do not want to farm the land but like to own it as a buffer for their farmhouses. One or two large, successful tenant-farmers who can make a go of it are still willing to rent their land. The result? A few ten-ants in a big way of business, and lots of small landlords.

I farm my view. We have two cottages that we let out by the week in the summer months, and I pay tribute to the many quiet couples who come here to birdwatch, walk, read or visit local beauty spots, and leave at the end of their week as tidily and unobtrusively as they have arrived. "What a wonderful view," they all exclaim when they climb out of their cars. In the village below, many of the old thatched cottages have gone the same way – let out by the week to holidaymakers. The village in winter has an empty, abandoned feel. The last dairy farmer in the village died a couple of years ago. His house was sold to a Londoner for a tidy sum. You would think that the summer letting market for Dorset cottages would be saturated by now. Every year more become available; every year they are fully booked.

The fall-out from foot-and-mouth last year was of course ghastly. There were no cases in Dorset – the nearest was 20 miles away in East Devon – but the countryside locked up its shutters and hid the key. All the markets were closed, and taking a lamb to the slaughterhouse became an obstacle-course of disinfection, permissions, and filling in forms. For me, 2002 has been the year of DEFRA paperwork. It feels at times as if I am standing beside a muckspreader spewing out ministry envelopes. DEFRA's directives arrive by almost every post. There are complicated rules to obey, it seems, and forms to be filled in, every time you turn a ewe over on its back. One of their most recent informed me that I am now, like much of England, in an NVZ (Nitrate Vulnerable Zone), and that I must keep precise records of stock movements in and out of every field – not just into and off the farm, as before – and of what fertiliser is applied to which field, how much, and when. If I do not, I face prosecution.

At the beginning of September, when the proposed Right to Roam maps for southern England were published on the Internet by the Countryside Agency, many an anxious farmer clicked his mouse on the screen. Inclusion in the green- or yellow-coloured areas would imply a plunge in his farm's amenity value by many thousands of pounds. It seemed so arbitrary. If you were on chalk, you were at risk; on acid, you probably got away with it. We are acid enough to grow rhododendrons here. We escaped for now, touch wood. It is hardly surprising that farmers like me feel that, in the government's and DEFRA's considered view, we are moral outlaws who need careful watching and control; soon to become actual outlaws if anti-hunting laws are passed and we get on our horses and ride behind a pack of hounds. (I am too creaky for that, but I object to being told what to do in matters of this kind.) On the Monday before the London march, as night fell, we lit a beacon on top of our hill, much as the Romans might have done 2,000 years before. The great semicircular ridge of hills that embosom Bridport and West Bay showed many affirming flames.

The march, in spite of attempts to make it appear so, was not a toff affair. It was palpably the yeomen of England on the move: tough, hard, uncompromising men who stood their ground with Cromwell, rather than charged with Prince Rupert's bluecoats, at Marston Moor; the sort of men to whom this country turns in times of danger and distress. They are a body of men and women whom our legislators ignore at their peril. They have been through the dark tunnel of farming recessions before, and emerged into the light. They will take on tendentious politicians, and win. They will keep on farming. I believe my West Dorset view will survive.

PETER ACKROYD

The rolling hills

MUCH OF THE ENGLISH LANDSCAPE STILL RISES AND declines in ancient patterns, which hold their own stories of lives laboriously led. The lines of ditches and hedgerows represent an ancient order, even densely built urban areas can reflect an older reality. Nineteenth-century Notting-ham, for example, was 'largely determined by the medieval footpaths and furlongs of the open fields'. It is an open secret that the topography of the City of London is estab-lished upon Roman and Saxon divisions. These affinities are not simply material for nostalgia, however. It is some-times supposed that landscape shapes human perception and that the power of the earth, the ground upon which we stand and move, is greater than that of the heavens in determining human destiny. Milton himself suggested that climate and topography nourish wit and consciousness as well as fruit, and more recent studies have confirmed the associations between locality and behaviour. It is of course a piece of ancient wisdom, but the present author has

[66]

noticed its workings in various districts of 21st-century London. It is the wisdom D. H. Lawrence gathered, and used, from the novels of Thomas Hardy in which "there exists a great background, vital and wild, which matters more than the people who move upon it."

Lawrence also said that Hardy's understanding of the world derived from his recognition of the territorial imperative and that "putting aside his metaphysic, which must always obtrude when he thinks of people, and turning to the earth, to landscape, then he is true to himself". It can be a source of power, too, as well as vision. As John Constable said of another country, "the Dutch were stay-at-home people. Hence their originality." But in England itself the source of that originality, or genius, may lie far back. The spires of 13th- and 14th-century parish churches, an example of a line of beauty in the English landscape, follow a geological stratum from Lincoln to north Somerset and seem ineluctably to rise out of oolite stone. Wordsworth pursues a similar course of enquiry when, in his *Guide Through the District of the Lakes*, he asks his reader to imagine a primitive landscape. "He may see or hear in fancy the winds sweeping over the lakes, or piping with a loud voice among the mountain peaks and, lastly, may think of the primaeval woods shedding and renewing their leaves with no human eye to notice, or human heart to regret or welcome the change." In the north-west region Wordsworth experienced "low breathings coming after him"; in that same territory, 500 years before, Sir Gawain felt "etins aneleden him", or giants blowing after him. The faint shudder of disquiet may be part of the landscape.

The coming of the Anglo-Saxons scarcely altered the vista of 'primaeval woods', with the ash and oak upon the

[67]

claylands and beech upon the chalk. Part of the country possessed a settled agrarian regime, inherited from Romano-British or prehistoric farmers. And many of the great forests had already been cut back or burned down. But much of England was still a wilderness covered with thick woods or with cold moorlands broken by outcrops of stone, marshlands, fens and heaths; log huts with thatched roofs betrayed their presence with thin plumes of smoke rising into the vast English sky, while in certain places the ruins left by earlier settlers were visible among the weeds and scrubland. Here, except for the wind sighing among the trees and the rain falling upon the damp soil, was silence – silence together with the calls of the natural world. Earnwood in Shropshire signifies 'eagle's wood', Yarnscombe in Devon means 'eagles' valley' and Arncliffe in Yorkshire 'eagles' cliff'. In these fastnesses we are not so far removed from the conclusion of *Wuthering Heights* with Heathcliff's headstone 'still bare' upon the moor. "I lingered round them, under that benign sky; watched the moths fluttering among the heath and hare-bells; listened to the soft wind breathing through the grass; and wondered how anyone could ever imagine unquiet slumbers, for the sleepers in that quiet earth." Here the protagonists have returned to the earth from which they came; after their fitful sojourn in the human world they have folded back into the landscape of which they were always a part.

This odd, silent and empty England in its earliest manifestations was one that haunted the Anglo-Saxon imagination. The opening encomia in the histories of Britain describe a landscape of springs and snow-white gravelled streams, of plains and hills and various flowers; but the imaginative work of the Saxons is possessed by cold and isolation and darkness. The female persona within one short poem laments her state of houselessness; she dwells within an ancient barrow among dark hills and dales. Guthlac fords a resting place upon a primeval mound or 'hill' within the wilderness. Everywhere there are references to steep and rugged places, to black waters and ice-cold streams, to crags and mountain caves. When Bede describes Ely as "an island surrounded by watery marshes" and Grantchester as "a small ruined city", he is describing a wasteland scarcely populated and meagrely cultivated, a darkly tangled landscape of wolves and boars. So it appears in *Beowulf*, too; the home of the monster race was the 'mor' and the 'faestnes', the moor and

the fastness where there is frost and darkness. It is the landscape of *King Lear* where "the wrathfull skies/Gallow the very wanderers of the darke" and the setting of *Sir Gawain and the Green Knight*:

Thay clomben bi clyffez ther clengez the colde...

Mist muged on the mor, malt on the mountez

Wild England is the context of the opening dream within *Piers Plowman*: "That I was in a wildernesse, wist I never where." It is couched in Hardy's *Far From the Madding Crowd* where "the general aspect of the swamp was malignant. From its moist and poisonous coat seemed to be exhaled the essences of evil things in the earth, and in the waters under the earth." It is the landscape that haunts the English imagination. Thus Egdon Heath, in Hardy's *Return of the Native*, "had a lonely face, suggesting tragical possibilities..."

Within the English landscape there are hallowed places, sacred by event or by association. There is a path that leads through English literature; it is the path of human agency and human settlement, a pact with the earth leading the traveller forward. It is the forest path, the wald-swathu, in *Beowulf*; it is the trackway along which Jude Fawley walks, weeping, in *Jude the Obscure*. John Clare rejoiced in "those crooked shreds/Of footpaths", of which Edward Thomas remarked that "the more they are downtrodden, the more they flourish"; they are themselves a sign or token of national feeling, like that long serpentine line which in *The Analysis of Beauty* William Hogarth named as the line of beauty. It is the line as curved or curling, in the sinuous grace of a reclining body or in a line drawn upwards around a cone, Hogarth simply called it "variety". Stanley Spencer's *The Bridlepath at Cookham* has the same irregular beauty as Paul Nash's *The Field Path*, both paintings showing narrow ways turning among fields and trees. The journey of Bunyan's Pilgrim, of Spenser's Red Crosse Knight, of Dickens's Little Nell, all take on the allegory of the winding path.

Since these are immemorial ways, a sense of custom is strongest; their presence may linger even after all outward marks have disappeared. The pathways of the Iceni lie beneath the crossroads of the Angel, Islington, in North London. These green lanes and narrow paths flourish in obscurity, sharing that privacy and inward shelter which are so much part of the English vision; they harbour, too, the sacredness of past associations which is also part of the vision. In E. M. Forster's *The Longest Journey* the path moves towards a circle of standing stones, suggesting the primal thread linking past and present times. Yet how quickly, too, that track can degenerate from a lane into an overgrown footpath as if it longed to return to desuetude and forgetfulness. John Cowper Powys, in the 20th century, invoked the sensations of walking in such a secluded place where "the spirit of the earth called out to him from the green shoots beneath his feet" so that he was filled with the *genius loci* and sustained by it. Here also he experienced "the innumerable personalities of all the men and women who for generations have gone up and down" these tracks across the earth. So the path may encourage moments of vision.

Keats knew in turn that "The poetry of earth is never dead." To be surrounded by the melody of landscape is to be blessed, to rest in the sleep of origins in which there is no difference between humankind and the natural world. The poetry and prose of the Anglo-Saxons are filled with the wonders of symbiosis. Bede, in his life of Cuthbert, relates how the saint walked down from his monastery to the adjacent sea; he knelt down upon the sand in prayer, whereupon two otters "bounded out of the water, stretched themselves out before him, warmed his feet with their breath, and tried to dry him on their fur". On another occasion some ravens pulled the straw from a hut which Cuthbert had built upon Farne Island, beside Lindisfarne; he reproved them and soon after one bird returned "with feathers outspread and head bowed low to its feet in sign of grief." The bird inhabited the small island also, and in the legends of English life power may reside in the most local circumstances. The site of the stream or 'borne' beside which Langland slumbered has been identified as the fountain of Malvern water which springs out of the west slope of the Herefordshire Beacon; the 'toure on the toft' is then the Norman castle immediately above it. The scene of Constable's *Autumn Sunset* is the footpath from East Bergholt Post Office to Stratford St Mary

Church, via Vale Farm. Blake's 'dark Satanic Mills' can readily be identified with the ruins of the Albion Mills along the Blackfriars Road, a short distance from Blake's house in Lambeth; he was the poet of eternity, but he identified himself with a local topography. These sites are irradiated by vision, but half their power derives from their particularity. On a larger scale, too, the country of England was considered to be charged with power. Saxton's county maps, published in 1579, provided the first complete set of visual images as fresh and illuminating to his first audience as photographs of the outer universe to a more recent generation. His work was complemented by Camden's *Britannia*, published seven years later, of which the purpose was 'to restore Britain to its Antiquities, and its Antiquities to Britain'. This was sacred soil indeed, hallowed by age and sanctified by association. Michael Drayton's *Poly-Olbion*, completed in 1622, is a poetic exercise in chorography, a great choral epic composed from 'the sundry Musiques of England'. In the 20th century Edmund Blunden compared the English landscape to a symphony. But by whom? By Vaughan Williams? Or Havergal Brian? For Drayton the music flows from the streams and rivers, such as the Severn and the Isis, while echoing among its hills and valleys. In the 12 maps which accompanied the first edition of *Poly-Olbion*, various shepherds, fairies and deities consecrate the land with "every mountain, forest, river, and valley, expressing in their sundry postures their loves, delights and natural situations"; the song of the earth is divinely ordered, and supplants the authority of the monarch or the newly emerging state. The 4,000 names inscribed upon Saxton's wall-map of England are a holy litany; as Drayton puts it, the "varying vein" of his poetical celebration registers the nature of "the varying earth". It is, once more, a highly localised vision like that of Blake or Langland.

Landscape began to emerge, in English painting, in the latter years of the 16th century and the beginning of the 17th century when various significant personages were placed in specific settings. This new imported form took so great a hold on the English imagination that it has ever since shared pre-eminence with portraiture as the great art of the nation. In a very English study of ruins Christopher Woodward has suggested that the "picturesque way of see-ing is arguably England's greatest contribution to European visual culture" and that the "picturesque remains an inseparable element of English taste", depen-dent upon individual memory and association rather than a theoretical aesthetic or codified practice.

In Jane Austen's *Emma* is depicted a view of gardens and meadows and avenues possessing "all the old neglect of prospect" – by which Austen means that the landscape had not yet suffered from the late 18th-century cult of the picturesque – but it still represented "English verdure, English culture, English comfort."

John Ruskin, with his acute sense of place, remarked that with the emergence of the landscape painter Richard Wilson in the 18th-century "the history of sincere land-scape art founded on a meditative love of nature begins in England." Yet love of nature is too crude or capacious a term to encompass the specific passion for the English countryside which animates the work of 18th- and 19th-century artists. There had been an attempt to translate the tenebrous mythologies of the French painters, Claude and Poussin, into the native English scene, but the indigenous taste for irregularity and contrast modified their lights and shades. Wilham Gilpin's *Observations on English Scenery*, published over a period of some 20 years at the end of the 18th century, digressed upon tones of air and earth "rarely permanent – always in motion – always in harmony – and playing with a thousand changeable varieties into each other". A contemporary, Uvedale Price, in turn advanced the beauties "of roughness and of sudden variation, joined to that of irregularity."

It cannot be the merest chance that these were also the qualities originally associated with English drama; it is as if national identity may be preserved in a thousand different guises. The emphasis is upon fluidity rather than formality, upon the manifestations of organic process rather than of any fixed design. All arts may in that sense concur. When Gainsborough turned his eyes away from the Suffolk landscape, his second passion was for music; Turner adored the poetry of James Thomson, whose *The Seasons* materially affected his art among 'the bright enchantment' and 'the radiant fields', the 'dewbright earth' and 'coloured air'. The painter also reflected that "painting and poetry, flowing from the same fount mutually by vision ... improve, reflect and heighten one another's beauties." Hardy's vision of landscape was profoundly influenced by Turner's paintings, which the novelist described as 'light modified by objects'. It is customary to ignore or neglect the sentiments of artists themselves, and to brook no association between poetry and painting, yet there is a connection and a continuity which have their origin in a distinctive English sensibility. Samuel Palmer was decisively influenced by the poetry of John Milton, and with his etchings illustrated *L'Allegro* and *Il Penseroso*;

all his life he tried to re-create the 'Valley of Vision' filled with the shadows cast by moonlight and the dark foliage of overhanging trees. And why should that sensibility not be nourished from childhood, or from memories beyond infancy itself? Constable confessed that "all that lies on the banks of the Stour... made me a painter" and that he painted "my own places best". Is it what Charlotte Brontë meant when she called her sister Emily "a native and nursling of the moors"?

Only the presence of some *genius loci* will explain the pre-eminence of the watercolour, for example, which has been described by one art historian as the 'medium peculiarly belonging to and expressive of the English spirit in art' with its velleities of atmosphere and moist air, with its almost melancholy sense of transience and of passage, with its evocation of broken light and fleeting shadow. The frontispiece of *Poly-Olbion* displays England draped across the image of a woman's body. In a similar spirit the American essayist, Washington Irving, once observed that the "pastoral writers of other countries appear as if they had paid nature an occasional visit and had become acquainted with her general charms; but the British poets have lived and revelled with her – they have wooed her in her most secret haunts – they have watched her minutest caprices." Not for the first time has the English landscape been compared to a human body. It is no allegory or personification, but a recognition of the landscape as an organic being with its own laws of growth and change.

This article is taken from Albion: The Origins of the English Imagination, *by Peter Ackroyd (Chatto & Windus, £25)*

MAX HASTINGS

Killing the countryside

IT WAS ANOTHER ROTTEN SUMMER FOR THE COUNTRYSIDE. Road-building returned to the centre of transport policy. Proposed reforms to the planning system were unveiled that seemed to be designed largely for the benefit of developers. There were various foot-and-mouth scares, most recently in St Cleer, Cornwall. The National Audit Office delivered a devastating report on fraud by farmers, vets and valuers during last year's foot-and-mouth outbreak. In West Berkshire, where I live, our neighbouring farmer is shutting down the dairy behind our house. Like most of his kind up and down the land, he is losing a fortune from milk production. Across Britain, we see the farming industry in desperate straits – and this time, it is a long-term trend, not a temporary hiccup – while the public's confidence in rural stewardship has never been lower. Housebuilders are intensifying pressure on the Government to release more agricultural land for building, and in many areas they face no resistance from farmers, eager to grab the cash. Laying concrete on fields is by far the most profitable activity in the British countryside today.

I live in the country, though like so many modern country-dwellers I earn my living from the city. Having given up editing newspapers after 16 years, it seemed about time to do something for a cause other than my own overdraft. When the Council for the Protection of Rural England asked me to become its president, I was flattered to accept. The council has been a conspicuous force for good in British life for 75 years. We can have an argument about where to place blame, but none at all about the fact that the countryside is in crisis. It seems a good moment for any of us able to contribute, even on the margin, to get out there and start pumping.

The CPRE's principal role is to campaign for how our countryside looks. Indeed, it plans to change its name from 'Council' to 'Campaign', because that best reflects what it does. But it is impossible to fight for green fields, hedgerows, and the rights of local communities to resist the relentless cupidity of developers, unless one also fights for the economic foundations of rural England.

It seemed right to abolish the name of the Ministry of Agriculture, a production-based body discredited by too many failures. But the creation of the Department for Farming and Rural Affairs is as much a waste of time as renaming the Post Office Consignia, unless it is matched by new ideas. In this as so much else, Labour has a sorry record of failing to match effective executive action to its well-meaning rhetoric. For half a century, farming was the most command-led industry in Britain. The legacy of food shortage in World War II was allowed to dominate policy for much too long. Today, we can see that the consequences for the environment, for consumers, and even for the long-term interests of farming were disastrous. I made a television documentary, *Cold Comfort Farm*, in 1985. Even then, it was easy to predict most of the misfortunes that have today befallen the countryside. All the sensible pundits could see them coming. Yet governments of all complexions did nothing. Above all, they failed to warn farmers and the public about the mounting crisis.

Today, it is widely accepted that farming must move from an agricultural subsidy system based on production, towards one that emphasises environmental good practice and social support, where this seems justified. But some politicians seem to share with many city-dwellers a belief that England can become a huge country park. In reality, while farming must change, it must also remain a profitable activity. Most of the countryside will remain a factory floor for food and natural fuel source production, even if this is conducted on a much more sensitive basis. It will be a tragedy if we end up with empty fields bereft of livestock, which is a serious threat. Our farming neighbour says that he is getting out of dairying not only because he is making no money, but also because he can no longer face the huge burden of regulation inseparable from keeping cows.

The CPRE is pressing for further reform of the dreaded Common Agricultural Policy, and for British Government policies which reflect the realities above. It is no longer possible to isolate rural development. We must see the countryside as an integral part of English life in making policy not only for the farming industry, encouraging diversification and environment-friendly activity, but also for transport and planning. The council is resisting proposals from government further to centralise the planning process. "Planning is the unsung hero of environmental protection, economic prosperity and the quality of life," says its commentary on the Government Green Paper. Government's intervention to curtail planning processes was prompted by the length and cost of the Heathrow Fifth Terminal Inquiry. Yet fewer than a dozen inquiries since 1984 have lasted more than three months. For the most part, the planning process works pretty well. It must remain the first line of defence against the housebuilders' lobby. Housebuilders do a vital job. But it is impossible to mask the fact that their objective is to maximise profit by gaining planning consents for new construction. They have no obligation to consider the interests of the countryside, or even of those who live in it, beyond their immediate customers. Government continues to confuse market demand for housing with housing need. New thinking – and more public money – is required to create 'affordable housing' in rural areas. It is essential to sustain emphasis on brownfield development, while resisting greenfield building. We are one of the most over-housed societies in the world, because of our distaste for living in extended families, and commitment to a universal right for each of us to occupy separate homes. Maybe this is what personal choice is about, but the price is high. One of the greatest ironies of English life is that we profess to love the countryside, yet we are killing it by inches.

Perhaps the most important job of the CPRE is to make government, and the public, stop and think before doing things which must blight the environment our descendants will inherit. Opposing relentless development is not nimbyism. CPRE's policy papers offer a coherent picture of what we should be doing, as well as what we should not.

As CPRE president, it is not my job to make the organisation's policy. Around the country, there is an army of CPRE volunteers, who monitor development, planning, transport and social issues, in the best traditions of voluntary service. The council's experts are then responsible for assessing their merits, carrying out research both local and national, then making a case to government and the media. If I can be of use, it is in giving a voice to some of these issues on behalf of the people doing the real work. Non-governmental organisations often find it hard to compete for space in print or on the air against the armoured divisions of Whitehall. Since words are my business, I hope I can provide some ammunition in the struggle. The English countryside is one of the most fiercely contested environments in the world. It is astonishing that so much of its beauty survives to this day, despite all the pressures. Our business is to see that it prospers into future generations, by showing government and the public some of the ways to avoid inflicting man-made disaster.

PEGGY VANCE

A countrywoman finds contentment again

ONE SPRING AFTERNOON, WHEN CLEARING OUT OLD papers from a drawer, Sussex farmer Reg Pritchard found a pair of smallish sketchbooks, beautifully bound in coarse linen. Despite the fierce sea breezes and salt mists of many coastal winters, they seemed to be in perfect condition, neither warped nor marked. Gently removing the old tie-bands, he opened the sketchbooks – and what he saw was quite incredible. Reg had stumbled upon the discovery of a lifetime. Brilliant butterflies, songbirds and seabirds, plants and seeds, bees and bugs teemed across the pages, each captured with the delicacy of a pressed flower. Here was Margaret Shaw's great secret, never revealed to him in the 15 years they had shared a home.

To Reg, Margaret was 'Auntie', a kindly friend 30 years his senior, and a countrywoman. In fact, Margaret Grace Shaw, photographed as a child by the Queen's photographer and a pupil at the select Cheltenham Ladies' College, had been born into a family of wealthy industrialists. Her grandfather, Matthew T. Shaw, owned the eponymous company, which had wharves and ironworks on the Isle of Dogs in East London. Around 1886, when Margaret was born, the increasing industrialisation of Victorian Britain led to an unprecedented demand for iron structures on a grand scale, and money poured into the family coffers. The Shaws bought yachts, travelled widely abroad, and, at the turn of the century, owned some of the earliest motor cars in Britain.

With her two older brothers, Godfrey and Guy, Margaret was very much a tomboy, swimming, riding and playing cricket to pass the long hot afternoons of summer. Their father, Harry, often joined their games, and Margaret adored him. In May 1902, when climbing a tree, she lost her footing and ended up, as her diary records, "hung elegantly" from a branch by the skirt of her gym dress: "I heard a tremendous clapping from father who said that he would come and photograph me if I did it again."

It would seem that Margaret's mother, Grace – the 'G.M.S.' so often mentioned in the journals – was equally loving and playful. Margaret records her mother's tendernesses, such as giving her not one but two bars of chocolate before her return to school. Margaret was always sad to leave her parents and, on Tuesday 25 June 1901, she noted: "Mother went this morning as I went to college. It was horrid to part after such a happy time... I have a lovely picture of mother and father for my birthday." At 15 Margaret seemed a most contented girl, well educated and in the heart of a loving family. In May 1901 the Shaws had moved from a sizeable country house, St Leonard's Grange in Beaulieu, to Selborne, 30 miles to the north-east, where they had bought The Wakes, a grand residence in which,

Selborne June. 1902.

Sunday 1st. Before breakfast took Father's photo in the garden with his camera. After breakfast went in the garden and got a ladder from the stable with the help of Uncle Ell, to get a rose from over the passage window. The ladder was very heavy & it was a very hot day. Then we looked round the garden for birds nests. Uncle Ell climbed the yew tree to see if he could find the nest out of which Leela took a poor little bird. He did not find it. We sat under the Douglas pine for some time, after which F.M & I came in to the drawing room and had our Service. Then we went out again. and "Booghe" and his daughter came. She is one of his ten daughters. He had one son who died when he was 2 years old. Theo

THE WAKES. SELBORNE.

Selborne June 1902.
daughter is called
Dolly. She paints
birds, for book illustrations;
and two of her sisters do the same, having
learnt from her. One sister has a lot to
do with African butterflies and is considered one of the best authorities on them.

CHURCH. SELBORNE. &c.

Miss Sharp thought
Leela was loo- dly
she is very
fond of cats.
After dinner we all
walked to Priory farm
going by the Lythe, which
is looking lovely. I walked chiefly
with Uncle Ell, & we looked for birds nests. As
we reached the farm we saw a swarm of
bees on the gate post, this is I believe the
first I have seen. The farm was rather
pretty. We walked through the yard, and
saw a darling little lamb there, it had
just been shorn, it got up and made

between 1728 and 1793, the naturalist, the Rev. Gilbert White, had lived and worked. It is now a well-known museum. Reg Pritchard is in no doubt that Margaret was profoundly influenced by the author of the famous *Natural History and Antiquities of Selborne*.

On moving into The Wakes her childhood diary blossoms with pressed pansies and wildflowers, and Saturday 31 May 1902 found her copying directly from Gilbert White: "After breakfast drew picture (& inked) of 'The Wakes' from G. White's book, in my Album." Margaret was an able student, ranked third in her class and top in Euclid studies; nevertheless, in keeping with a young lady's syllabus of the time, she spent much of the school day sketching and painting. Classes in perspective, 'heads' and drawing were complemented by her own passion for nature, and the observations in the diary of her youth sound remarkably like those of her later journals: "... we looked for birds' nests. As we reached the farm we saw a swarm of bees on the gate post, this is I believe the first I have seen. The farm was rather pretty. We walked through the yard and saw a darling little lamb there, it had just been shorn..." (June 1902.)

Here already is the detail and tenderness that infuses all Margaret Shaw's writings. She cherished animals of all kinds, and her journals repeatedly bear witness to her efforts to protect even the smallest creatures. Aged 40 she was no less compassionate than at 15. On 5 November 1926 she noted: "A Small Tortoiseshell Butterfly flew round our heads at breakfast, and finally alighted on the floor, where I was only just in time to rescue it from the cats. I carried it to my South window, where it sunned itself all day, wandering up and down the panes, with widespread wings. Each time I attempted to let it out, it folded its wings tightly and refused to move, so I let it stay in the warm."

Polly the parrot, Algy the goat, Sally the donkey, Barney the dog and Nicco the cat – the latter much chastised for his murderous ways – were just some of the much-photographed pets on which Margaret lavished her affections over the years. Her concern for animals suggests that Margaret would have been a doting mother, but she never married, and, to Reg Pritchard's knowledge, was never courted. Her maternal instincts were directed instead towards her young cousins, Norah and Mary, who came to live with Margaret in the early 1930s, and whom she treated like daughters, allowing them many privileges. Mary was keen on riding, so lessons were organised with Miss Somerville, who owned a riding school in Haslemere. When, in the mid 1940s, the school came up for sale, Margaret Shaw very generously bought it for Mary, and farmer Reg Pritchard, who lived nearby, was invaluable in helping run the fledgling business.

Reg, who had struggled desperately to make ends meet during the devastating depression in farming, was run off his feet keeping his farm going, helping with the stable and trying to look after his retarded brother. Seeing his dedication – and his exhaustion owing to the illness and recent death of his mother – Margaret Shaw made an extraordinary offer: to keep house for him and work on the farm. So it was that Reg became her adopted 'nephew' and in 1949, aged 63, 'Auntie Shaw' moved into the farmhouse that was attached to Reg's farm, near Haslemere.

By that time Margaret had lost her brother Godfrey (who had been killed in India), her parents, and latterly

Norah, whose unexpected death she had taken extremely badly. Clearly, with no occupation, so much personal grief to bear and old age looming, Margaret was keen to find a place and a purpose for the final chapter of her life. The transition was nonetheless dramatic. How many women of Margaret Shaw's class and background would have been adaptable enough to swap the life of a privileged country lady for that of a toiling countrywoman? In place of extensive travels, visits to the opera, entertaining and passing the time with literature and games, from 1949, at Reg's farm, Margaret made up the workers' pay packets, helped keep the books, collected the eggs, cared for Reg's brother, and worked ceaselessly for the benefit of the farm.

Margaret's journals of the 1920s were completed long before this transformation, but in many ways anticipate it. In undertaking the diaries Margaret set herself a daunting challenge. Watercolour is well known to be the most unforgiving medium – blotches cannot be erased or mistakes corrected – and, with great daring and dedication, Margaret chose to paint her finely executed images directly into the sketchbooks. Each page had to be perfect or the book would be ruined. Had Margaret been producing quick sketches, she could have worked directly from life, but with many of the subjects she chose to illustrate, she would have had only brief sightings. She needed to make a quick identification and then either paint from memory or use a book illustration as an aide-memoire. She was certainly well read in natural history, but looking up, identifying and copying so many different creatures would have required tireless dedication, especially at a time when there was little colour reference available.

There is no snobbery in the journals. While it is clear

from the various locations in which she worked – including Scotland, Wales, France and Italy – that Margaret had wonderful opportunities for travel and leisure, she was as careful in the painting of a common daisy as in the depiction of more rare and exotic discoveries.

Where Margaret's early diary hummed with people, in the later journals humans are barely in evidence. Margaret's mother and father appear infrequently as 'G.M.S.' and 'H.T.S.', and then only to kill a wasp or feed a bird. The journals are instead peopled by animals; 'Mr Sparrow' and 'Mr Nuthatch' are spotted on 25 March 1928 and 'Mr G.S.W.' – Great Spotted Woodpecker – and his daughter on 9 July of that year. So exclusively does Margaret focus on nature that even the Christmas period goes unremarked, save for the making each year of a tree decorated with food for the birds.

In her journals Margaret could escape the strictures of class and society. The animals are her dramatis personae, whose antics she watches day by day and records in detail. On 6 August 1927 she observes a confrontation: "This morning a wasp got entangled in a spider's web on my window. The spider darted out, but was afraid to venture too near, and the next moment the wasp had freed itself and flown away. The spider retired discomfited." There is no pretension in the writing. With the instincts of a true naturalist, she notes down whatever she finds interesting, including more unusual animal behaviours. On 19 July 1927 she was by Dunnet Head lighthouse in the north of Scotland, watching the seabirds: "I saw a Lesser Black Backed Gull, the lighthouse man told us they are regular thieves, and go round turning other birds off their eggs. As a rule the eggs never fall off the ledges they are laid on, being shaped so that they only revolve but never roll, but he has seen the sitting bird pull the egg off the rock with her when attacked by the L. Black Backed Gull."

Nowhere are the journals a dry record; throughout they are infused with an infectious enthusiasm. Every sun-dappled day and starlit night is celebrated, and Margaret has a warm descriptive voice that makes for an evocative read: "Great Tits were very busy climbing about the dejected rose bushes." (12 November 1927.) "Dogs' eyes in the dark, when the car lights shine upon them are like tiny round phosphorescent lamps – some glowing red, some green." (16 December 1927.) "Frog spawn in the upper ponds has hatched and there is a dense mass of wriggling blackness." (18 March 1928.)

In Shaw's bucolic world the eaves swarm with House Martins, elm trees still grow tall, and the hedgerows are full of "quarrelsome, noisy wrens". What she so poignant-ly captures is the last of a Britain unspoiled by prairie fields and intensive crop-spraying. Here is the country as we would wish it today – fertile, varied and picturesque. Margaret had an eye for landscape in all weathers and colours: "a glorious sunrise" in Sussex; "a slight fog" in London; and "sullen skies with angry clouds" in the Highlands of Scotland. Watercolour vignettes in her jour-nals capture the most attractive of these scenes. A keen photographer, Margaret often made the landscape her subject, composing images that are strikingly profession-al. Margaret Shaw was an artist, a naturalist and a writer, but equally she was an inspired and witty designer. Each page of the journal is carefully laid out, and in places Margaret reveals an almost modern design sensibility. Pleasing visual conceits enliven many of the pages: on 17

March 1927 the starlings rise up in a great arc, scattering the text; heavy rain pours right through 1 July 1927, "The wettest day of the year;" and autumn leaves fall across a whole page, from 16 to 20 October 1927.

In everything she did Margaret was creative. Whether painting, embroidering or cooking, she was a perfectionist, always trying to do her best and make the most of her materials. Margaret shared Reg's love of labour and, on Reg's mother's death, helped Reg build his farm into a business so successful that, by September 1955, Reg and Margaret were able to retire to a four-acre seaside estate in West Sussex.

Now in his eighties, Reg recalls the contentment he and Margaret found in each other's company: "She worked very hard, but she found happiness again. In fact we were both extremely content. I think we shared the belief that there was only one way to do a job: perfectly." For Margaret it was the ideal retirement, free from worldly cares, at one with the land and the sea, and in a newly minted family: Reg and the wildlife around them. The Margaret Shaw of *A Countrywoman's Journal* had found her natural home.

A facsimile edition of Margaret Shaw's A Countrywoman's Journal *is published by Constable & Robinson, £12.99. To order a copy at the special price of £10 (incl p&p), telephone 01206 255800 and quote the reference 'Countryman'. Offer ends 20 December 2002.*

RICHARD MABEY

Badlands made good

IN 1668 THE NORFOLK VILLAGE OF SANTON DOWNHAM was buried under a sandstorm, a blow-out from an inland dune system at Lakenheath Warren, a few miles to the south. It was, by any reasonable English standards, an outlandish occurrence. But this was the Breckland, 'a vast Arabian desert' straddling the Norfolk-Suffolk borders which had long been notorious with travellers. Many used to cross 'the horrible Brandon sands' in the dawn to avoid upsetting the horses, and there was a kind of wooden lighthouse to guide anyone unfortunate enough to be benighted. Seven years after the Santon storm the diarist John Evelyn noted that "the Travelling Sands have so damaged the country, rolling from place to place, and quite overwhelmed some gentlemen's estates", and he urged them to plant "tufts of firr" to stabilise the sand.

They didn't need much encouragement. As the fashion for improvement gathered pace during the late 18th and 19th centuries Breckland landowners went in for all manner of schemes to make their local wilderness bear fruit. They planted thickets for pheasants, turnips to enrich the soil and pine hedges to check the winds. Eventually – with more than a suggestion that poetic justice had been done – Santon Downham rose again as the local headquarters of the Forestry Commission, whose vast pine plantations had become the biggest single enterprise to keep the sand in its place. In the 1940s Lakenheath Warren vanished under the runways of an airfield (now a US base). In the 1970s and 1980s all the remaining open dunes were tidily fenced off and labelled as nature reserves. Breckland has been very nearly brought to heel, and for the first time not everyone feels comfortable about this particular triumph of man over waste.

For much of its recent history, Breckland has been regarded as a classic piece of wasteland, somewhere to lose unpopular and land-hungry activities like battle-training and commercial forestry. There weren't many other obvious uses for an infertile plain which had the lowest rainfall in Britain, and which was almost devoid of the features usually regarded as making a picturesque landscape. I doubt if there is another comparable tract of rural England (it covers some 400 square miles, from Bury St Edmunds in the south to Swaffham in the north) that is so little known and so impatiently rushed through by travellers. When I first began exploring East Anglia 40 years ago it felt like an occupied zone, an intimidating gauntlet of barricaded shooting estates and military bases. Yet everywhere there were reminders of the old waste clinging on in the margins. You could pick up neolithic arrowheads in the fields. Species of wild flower grew on the road verges that didn't crop up again until you reached the East European steppes.

Nightjars seemed to find echoes of their ancestral habitats in the new forestry clearings, and churred in ever increasing numbers through the summer dusks. I began to find modern Breckland a haunting and evocative place, a ghost of the old landscape of immense sandy heaths and stony scrubland, and when dust-devils were whirling across the carrot fields and through the stunted pine wind-breaks it did not seem implausible that flocks of great bustard stalked the plains only 150 years ago.

Given the seemingly run-down state of the place, it was a rather perverse fascination. But attitudes towards landscape change, and just as it seemed to be on its last legs, the Breckland has come into its own. It has even received the ultimate tribute of having a District Council named after it. A better guide to its status may be the changing patterns of land-use, in which both the leisure industry and low-intensity farming have made strong showings. The annual tally of visitors to the Forestry Commission's Thetford Forest Park has passed the 1.5 million mark. Center Parcs have one of their holiday villages in a pine plantation on the Iveaghs' estate at Elveden. And in 1988, in a move that challenged the assumptions of underlying centuries of agricultural development, the Government designated the region as an Environmentally Sensitive Area (ESA), in which farmers are encouraged to return to methods which will conserve historic or locally distinctive landscapes.

The scheme has worked quite well. But if some farmers were initially doubtful about taking part it wasn't simply that they were unimpressed by the scale of grants and compensation. To *not* improve their land, to deliberately court infertility, went against a whole tradition of husbanding instincts. But the argument is nothing like as black-and-white as plenty versus barrenness, and the example of the Breckland may have something to teach us about a discriminating attitude towards fertility.

But there is no avoiding the fact that the Breckland is a prime home-grown example of what deforestation can lead to. Up to a couple of hundred years ago it was the nearest thing Britain had to a dust-bowl. In parts this may have been its natural state. The area is defined by deposits of sand and gravel that were washed here by glacial melt-waters, and there may have been areas of especially loose sand on exposed ridges that never sustained a permanent woodland cover. But most of the open areas were created or encouraged by human activity. The light soils made forest clearance easy, and in prehistoric times it was one of the most densely populated areas of Britain. Grazing by semi-domesticated cattle would soon have converted what remained of the woodland to a mixture of wiry grass and heather. A large and sprawling network of trackways and drove roads connected the region with the Icknield Way and trading settlements on the East Anglian coast.

Among the most important items of trade ferried along these tracks were worked flints, for use in knives, weapons and farm implements. Flint is abundant throughout East Anglia, but Breckland had some of the best quality, and became a centre for flint-knapping skills. At Grimes Graves just north of Brandon, there is a prehistoric flint-mine in which well over 500 shafts have been uncovered.

Early farming itself was a less rewarding business. The thin soils soon began to lose their fertility, and at some unspecified date the system that eventually gave the region its name evolved. A field would be cultivated for a few years and then abandoned for as many as 20 to give it time to recover. These long-term fallow plots were named after an Old English term, brek, meaning a tract of land broken up for cultivation and then allowed to revert. You can glimpse what these archaic stony plots were like in parts of Weeting and Thetford Heath National Nature Reserves. Sheep-grazing was the most sensible use for both the grasslands and the brecks, and large flocks were roaming the region by Roman times. In the Middle Ages they were joined by rabbits, which were kept in enormous high-banked warrens. By the middle of the 18th century, there were reckoned to be more than 15,000 acres of organised warren in the Brecks, and the traveller and agricultural reporter Arthur Young (1741-1820) quoted the figure of 40,000 rabbits as the production of just one warren.

At this time Breckland was probably as wild and inhospitable as it has ever been, with the areas of eroded sand growing as grazing pressure increased. This was the heyday of the exploration of Britain, and inquisitive travellers like Young, William Gilpin, the antiquarian Dr Stukeley and Charles Kidman all visited the region. Almost without exception they regarded it as loathsome and treacherous. Only the Duc de La Rochefoucauld, a waspish 18-year-old French nobleman who toured East Anglia in 1784, saw some merit in the place – in the rabbits if nothing else. Commenting on the landscape between Bury and Thetford, he wrote: "The whole of the country through which the road runs for a distance of eight miles is covered with heather in every direction as far as the eye can see... no trees, no cultivation, everywhere sand, everywhere little clumps of reeds and bracken. A large portion of this arid country is full of rabbits, of which the numbers astonished me. We saw whole troops of them in broad daylight and we could almost touch some of them with our whips. I enquired the reason for this prodigious number and was told that there was an immense warren which brought in 200 guineas a year to the owner. The dry sand which pervades the district militates against improvements and I do not believe that it will ever be possible, in such an unfavourable soil, to put the 20 miles of country which we covered in the course of the day under cultivation."

In this he underestimated the ingenuity and ambition of the local squires. During the early years of the 19th century the farming systems of the Breckland were totally transformed. Between 1800 and 1820, 49 Parliamentary Enclosure Acts took in nearly 120,000 acres of grass and heathland. Common rights were extinguished and the rabbit warrens abolished. Pine wind-breaks – cut back like hedges to encourage lateral growth – made their appearance (and produced such distinctive rows of contorted trees that now, ironically, they are regarded as crucial elements in the 'landscape heritage'). Increasingly, the small farms were bought out by the large landowners, a process which accelerated once the great agricultural depression had set in in the 1870s. Breckland became a region of vast private estates – Elveden, Euston, Culford, West Stow, Stanford – many of them more than 10,000 acres in extent and able to turn the slump to their advantage by using their rough land for raising pheasants. Breckland became for a while the pheasant-shooting centre of England, and was the site of some terrible *battues*. The Maharajah Duleep Singh, who rebuilt Elveden into a passable imitation of a north Indian palace in 1870, once slaughtered 789 partridges in a single day. Tom de Grey, the sixth Lord Walsingham, used to go shooting dressed in a snakeskin waistcoat and a hat made from a whole hedgehog. On a winter's day in 1889, in the marshy heathland round Stanford, he bagged 65 coots, 39 pheasants, 23 mallard, seven teal, six gadwall, four pochard, one goldeneye, three swans, three snipe, one woodcock, one pigeon, two herons, two moorhens, 16 rabbits, nine hares, one otter, one pike (shot underwater) and a rat. Game shooting continues in the Brecks, and has left some unhappy local legacies, not least a rather cavalier attitude towards bird protection laws and an entrenched hostility towards public access. But once farming became prosperous again after the war, landowners returned to the business of improving their cultivated areas. Now the sandy soils grow high quality carrots and asparagus, and much of the cultivation is sub-contracted out to specialist growers, who undertake the whole business from sowing to harvesting.

Bill Nickson, the DEFRA Project Officer for the Breckland ESA, keeps a personal copy of the Ministry of Agriculture's journal for May 1952 (his birth month) as a benchmark against which to measure changing attitudes. It contains an exhortation from the then Minister, Thomas Dugdale, to produce more food from our own soil, and a book review of *The Elveden Enterprise* which described enthusiastically how a large part of this Breckland estate had been converted from the heath. "They were responding to the needs of their time, just as they are now," he told me a few years ago. The needs of the time now are seen in terms of the preservation of the heathland and the fallow 'brecks', and Bill is empowered to offer grants to farmers for various initiatives aimed at meeting these objectives. Within a year of Breckland's designation as an ESA, there were agreements for the conservation of 1,300 hectares of heath and dry grassland, in which farmers agree to restrict their use of pesticides and fertiliser and manage the grass by grazing. Further agreements encouraged rough flower-rich strips at the edges of arable fields, but the option of allowing arable fields to revert to fully-fledged brecks has been slower to catch on. Despite many successes, there are still vast tracts of the Breckland which are impervious to current ideas about conservation and access. And in the wake of the rabbit and pheasant there is now a third generation of Breckland sporting beast: the thoroughbred horse. The new stud farms, done up with neo-classical porticos and smart post-and-rail fences, stand out like South Forks in the tousled Breck prairieland.

But you get used to incongruous sights. A few years ago, I was up there in the early summer, and the new unsprayed field-edges, full of mignonette and poppies, were also bristling with soldiers in camouflage. It was the middle of a big NATO exercise, and I was rather lucky to get a guided trip round the Stanford Battle Area from Bob Berry of the Property Services Agency (PSA). Berry showed me hardwood plantings deliberately edged with scrub and cleared pine plantations that they were attempting to return to a heather cover. The sheep that graze much of the 17,000 acres of land are worked according to the upland hefting system, in which small, clannish flocks graze their own patch of territory and need the minimum of shepherding. The local birds seemed ineffably unconcerned about the furious activity involved in the exercise. Swallows commuted to nests in old pillboxes. Two curlews did a display flight around a low-flying helicopter. It turned out that the camp commandant was also chairman of the Stanford conservation group, and was in the habit, during the lambing and nesting season, of putting out radar traps to catch speeding tanks. Wargames are not always played by such sentimental rules.

We drove up to the highest point in the Battle Area, Frog Hill. The view over miles of pale, stony grassland, studded with pine and scrub, is extraordinary, like nothing else in this country except perhaps the New Forest. You can just catch glimpses of Langford, Stanford and Tottington churches, all that remains of the villages that were appropriated to create the Battle Training Area during World War II. As in many similar areas, the army promised that the villagers could return after the ceasefire. It never happened, and the only way the dwindling number of surviving inhabitants can return to their birthplace is to be buried there.

Only on the Forestry Commission's land is one free to walk about at will in the Brecks. This was one of the first areas to be planted up by the Commission in its post-Great War mission to increase the nation's strategic timber reserve. Now it is the largest single landowner in Breckland, with 21,000 hectares. Most of this is planted up with Corsican pines, which for decades put the countryside here under a forbidding and monotonous drape. But as the earlier plantings have come round for felling, the landscape has become perceptibly more open. The Forestry Commission is also now committed to promoting nature conservation and public enjoyment of its estates, and nowhere is this policy more evident than the Brecks. There are nature trails and a red squirrel project, and the Forest Park, which includes a fair amount of the commercially worked area.

On some sites the Commission has created unusually large clear-fells of up to 30 hectares, for reasons that have little to do with timber management. Beyond Emily's Wood, north of Brandon, the aim is to give travellers along the A1065 an idea of what the open prospects of Breckland might once have looked like, stretches of rough land clear to the tree belts on the horizon. Down in Wangford Warren there is an immense clearing specifically for the benefit of nightjars, woodlarks and hunting goshawks. (I once saw a sign outside the nearby farm which announced, with typical local opportunism, 'Goshawks!', as lesser holdings do their honey and free-range eggs.)

Meandering between these forest clearings, watching the tree pipits doing their melodramatic free-fall song-flights, was the pleasantest part of that visit. And at night, with the vegetation underfoot smelling of fern and foxes, and the nightjars gliding out like ghostly kites against the silhouetted trees, there was a palpable sense of the old wilderness. But much of the rest of Breckland seemed to have become a curmudgeonly and inhospitable place. There was almost nowhere to walk. The network of ancient tracks that pass across the estates south of Elveden were blocked by curt 'Private' signs. Even England's oldest road, the Icknield Way, summarily peters out once it leaves the Forestry Commission's Kings Forest. I began to wonder if the time might not be approaching when, in the public interest, the whole of Breckland should be looked on – and administered – as a national asset.

My private dream – of the army leaving Stanford to become England's first American style 'roadless area' – will probably remain a fantasy. But public opinion is changing. More than a century ago, in his extraordinary description of the Dorset heathland in *The Return of the Native*, Thomas Hardy predicted that: "The New Vale of Tempe may be a gaunt waste in Thule: human souls may find themselves in closer and closer harmony with external things wearing a sombreness distasteful to our race when it was young." It would no longer seem out of place for the Breckland to become an Area of Outstanding Natural Beauty, or even a lowland National Park. For some years now, such possibilities have been whispered behind closed doors among those many conservation groups that, increasingly, keep an eye on the region's ecological health. There is a belief that the place has been over-grazed and over-manured, and that perhaps what is needed is a return to the old breck system itself – cultivation followed by a long fallow period. It is, ironically, a system that the much-abused Forestry Commission are already almost following. Their policy of short-term rotations followed by large clearances is like a condensation of the prehistoric farming systems here. If they could be persuaded to allow longer periods before replanting they might produce a model for the Brecks, a landscape that, as Hardy put it, was "impressive without showiness, emphatic in its admonitions, grand in its simplicity". And, alternating forest with fallow, it would also be a salutary place for meditating upon the fact that fertility is not something that can be endlessly exploited without, so to speak, a break.

A collection of Richard Mabey's writing, Country Matters, *is published by Pimlico, £12.50.*

NATHALIE CURRY

Why can't it be a heaven on earth?

HE IS MUCH, MUCH SMALLER THAN I IMAGINED. PERHAPS television exaggerates the image as it does the personality. Here in the flesh he seems half lost in his armchair. The big bushy white beard and the billowing eyebrows are real, though, as are the craggy lines that score his forehead, a legacy of over 40 years on the campaign trail. But the handshake is almost limp, far from the firm grasp for which I had braced myself. Instinctively I look at his hands, expecting to see those of a botanist, with earth locked beneath the fingernails and the skin calloused and abrasive from years of being plunged into the soil. But his hands are on the small side, and almost feminine. His voice is muffled and gruff, the words struggling through the beard which entirely conceals his mouth. It's his trademark voice, but lower and softer. I have to strain to catch what he is saying.

"I am actually a very shy, private person," David Bellamy confesses. "I get terrible butterflies when I have to stand up in front of a group of people and really have to hype myself up." Not, I think to myself, the impression you get from the television. He seems to read my thoughts: "David Bellamy becomes a belligerent person when on screen," he asserts. Indeed, he thinks his forthrightness may have something to do with the fact that he has not been on screen since 1996. "When my mind gets going it says what it wants to say. I am not careful about what I say, which is why I have been banned off the telly."

There can't be many personalities who made their television debut standing on a mussel-encrusted pipe that was discharging raw sewage into the sea near Redcar. But Bellamy did, shortly before an oil slick off the Cornish coast in 1967 led to a media hunt for someone who could talk about marine pollution – at which point Bellamy, a lecturer in botany at Durham University, found himself in sudden demand. He has been a celebrity ever since, although he only resigned his position at Durham (after 22 years) in 1982. He still remembers the one-liner which set him upon his television career: "You see what is coming out of the end of that pipe," he told his unseen audience. "It may be shhhhh, you know what, to you and me, but to a mussel that's cordon bleu cookery." Since then he has made more than 40 television series and videos and become President or Vice President of 43 non-governmental organisations around the globe.

He has spent his winters studying coral reefs in the Indian Ocean and his summers in the high Arctic. He almost died from a bush spider bite followed by a bout of malaria on a field trip to the tropical rainforests of Sierra Leone and was arrested and gaoled on his 50th birthday whilst campaigning to stop the building of a hydro-electric dam in Tasmania. He has written 43 books, of which the latest is his autobiography *Jolly Green Giant*. Is jolliness Bellamy's defining trait, then? He says the fictional character he would most like to be is Tolkien's Tom Bombadil from *The Lord Of The Rings*, the hopping and dancing merry master of wood, water and hill. But if anything permeates his autobiography it is not a jovial optimism but rather a persistent strain of nostalgia that borders on melancholy. He thinks modern Britain has lost the diversity and community spirit that he remembers from his childhood. "Children don't have childhoods any more. Where do children play?" he asks me. "We have plastic pubs which all sell the same beer. Children go to the play booth inside for their parties or the swings outside which look like trees out of *Alice in Wonderland*. When I was a kid I was never at home. I was finding things out and learning. The milk was still delivered on a milk float with a horse pulling it. You would help the milkman; you knew the farmer; it was wonderful. It was a childhood spent outdoors, not stuck in front of the telly or the computer. We had our roots in real people."

He is leaning forwards now, sitting on the edge of the chair, animated and cupping his hands together in a gesture that I recognise from the television. His pale blue eyes, hidden behind heavily hooded lids, are suddenly excited. "We were not battery people living caged in houses and cars," is how he sums it up in his book. "My Play Station was the freedom of the parks and the informal green space which included bomb sites in which nature had found new habitats." Bellamy was born and brought up in Surrey "when it was still the countryside", in a strict Baptist family. His father's career as a pharmacist for Boots Cash

Chemists took the family from a rented semi in Carshalton to a brand new Potterton house in Cheam. He remembers the constant fear of Doodlebugs that fell over Cheam on their way to London, and the nightly spectacle of the Blitz clearly visible from their house on the London skyline.

But is this nostalgia a sense of a lost childhood or more of a lost world? Bellamy does not seem to draw a distinction. "We had farmers who talked about keeping their soil in good heart to hand on to their children as a viable industry. If you went into a Somerset pub, they talked with a Somerset accent and they did things the Somerset way. Britain was a small bite-sized place where you could go from culture to culture, and the countryside reflected that culture." As he gets into his conversational stride, I see a little more of the belligerent, small-screen Bellamy. He prods me repeatedly as he speaks, pushing his points home. "I could get on my bike and cycle from London to Brighton to see the sea. It was bursting with biodiversity. There were small farms surrounded by hedgerows, small estates with very good gamekeepers,and the proletariat who had rats in their cellars understood that you had to kill things."

The childhood images come back again and again. They seem to have an almost sacred energy for him. He recalls his discovery of botany in a woodland glen near Midhurst in Kent as a "spiritual orgasm"; and, six decades later, nature is clearly still much more than just 'the environment' for Bellamy. It is a personal and religious experience. "It was my road to Damascus," he says now of that first conversion. "I remember sitting down in the wood at the age of eight or nine and thinking what an amazing place this is. I used to dam the streams for fish and was surrounded by flowers. I thought this is what they are talking about at Sunday school. It's creation." So how has that creation altered since then? Bellamy's answer is emphatic. The extensive changes to the British country-side in his lifetime have not just made his work as a botanist harder but also affected him personally. Thus he is unwilling to return to that woodland glen of his child-hood for fear of what he might, or might not find.

"There are no more flowers to study," he says sadly. "Rural England has disappeared and has been replaced by four million hectares of broad-acre farmland. At the end of the war, 130,000 miles of hedgerows were torn down and 98 per cent of our flower rich grasslands were wiped over. All this has raised the score of many of our common plants, birds and animals ever upwards on the scale of rar-ity. Vibrant villages have become sleepy dormitories. Urban greenspace where I used to pick wildflowers for my mum is now covered with concrete. Bluebell woods that were once a cycle ride away from central London have become part of open fields drenched with fertiliser. Temperatures are going up. Birds are coming in earlier. They're nesting earlier and they're fledging earlier. The seasons have all moved up three months. We don't really have a winter any more, but April showers seem to happen in June and July, then the summer is pretty wet and miserable."

Bellamy's preferred solution would be integrated crop management, a low input farming system which seeks to harness biodiversity to promote crop production, with uncultivated 10-metre headlands surrounding fields, strips of perennial wild flowers, and hedgerows which can provide habitat for insects and birds, thus restoring the natural predatory cycle of the countryside. "It puts insects and birds back where they should be and uses a third less chemicals. It brings back the skylarks and butterflies. I can show you farms where farmers using integrated crop management have made more profit because they have used less fertiliser. "My point is straightforward. A farmer needs to understand that he is going to make a living, not a killing. He needs to get to the stage where he asks himself how fast the wind is blowing today and decides that he won't spray." Bellamy pauses, looking around the room, and pulls hotly at the neck of his mustard-coloured T-shirt. "Whenever I talk like this people tell me that this is utopia," he complains. "But why shouldn't we be thinking of a heaven on earth?" His vision of the future is, he hopes, a relatively practical utopia. He is in favour of motorways and railways when built in the right places, for example, and he also backs caravans, so that people can feel grass beneath their feet. "It would be a very, very hi-tech countryside with extremely good public transport, where we could feed ourselves mainly. We would have rivers full of fish, salmon back in the numbers they were. Every child could pick a bunch of wildflowers for their mum on her birthday, or for the church on Sunday. It's easy. That is all easy to do."

But although he has some faith in the ability of mankind to undo some of its environmental mistakes, Bellamy admits to getting very depressed sometimes at the way things are going – at which point he comforts himself by watching a *Swallows and Amazons* video. There is, I realise, something quite vulnerable about him, weary even. We talk about his lost childhood again and the influence that Arthur Ransome's books had on his life. His head seems to sink into his shoulders. "They were all about kids trying to stop people from destroying things," he laments. "Kids can't get into a boat now and sail out to an island because someone's built on their island already."

For Bellamy and his wife, Rosemary, whom he married in 1959, children matter very much. They lost five children in succession but now have five, four of whom are adopted. "We always said we'd adopt two and have two, because when we got married there were too many people in the world. But we ended up with one and adopted four." His greatest achievements, he says, are his grandchildren. David Bellamy looks tired. He was up at 6am today and 4am yesterday and had two sleepless nights before that. He is not expecting to spend another day at home – near Hamsterley in County Durham – for more than two months. Instead, he will travel around the world four times, visiting Java, Australia, New Zealand and Canada en route. Apart from promoting his autobiography at home, he is also awaiting the launch of his newest book, on world herbal medicine, while working on another, which proposes a new theory of evolution.

He is 69 – 70 in January – and says he will not contemplate retirement before 90. "I could spend my whole life and not know very much about Britain. There are so many things that one wants to do and can do. My granny said that if you lived the good life, you would go to heaven for ever. But I don't want to go to heaven for ever. I mean, how boring. What would I do? What happens to all the ideas I've had? What happens to the memory of me sitting here talking to you? I've been a good liver, but I am going to be an awful dier."

David Bellamy's autobiography, Jolly Green Giant, *is published by Century (£16.99).*

[109]

DAVID WALKER

The Woodchester Chronicles

THOSE OF MY GENERATION WHO WERE 'WAR CHILDREN' IN London and other vulnerable cities often owe their survival to evacuation: I was such a child. During the Blitz, in exchange for my natal home of Hounslow, I was fortunate to live with real relations in the South Cotswold parish of Woodchester, near Stroud in Gloucestershire. My first memories of Woodchester originate from this time, when Larchgrove Cottage became my haven: listening to the Home Service on a crystal set, flying a model glider on Rodborough Common, and with my aunt on Selsley Common gleaning barley after the harvest to feed her hens; for in the war years, part of the common was ploughed up to help feed the nation. I also remember attending the local primary school, where, by today's standards, I would have got a grade 'A' for dreaming. Then, after the war, I returned many times on a Great Western steam train, the Cheltenham Flier, being seen off by my father at Paddington station. Here, as when I had been evacuated, I was placed 'in care of the guard'. Today, I suspect even an inanimate object would be at high risk. I continued to visit Woodchester as a teenager in the 1950s, unconsciously imbibing more of its natural history, often in the company of like-minded mates I had known since evacuation days. They had already introduced me to the delights of their 'home range', such as exploring the Dingle, or building a dam across its stream, setting up headquarters in a red-brick barn (when farmer Fawkes's bull was not at home), and fossil-hunting on Selsley Common. They also showed me how to smoke the dried stems of wild clematis, or traveller's joy, which they called 'blithytwine', until I became dizzy; but I didn't smoke it long enough to become addicted.

Later, after university and employment, marriage and children, I tended to drift away from my Woodchester mates during visits, for they had gone their separate ways; and there was no more smoking of the weed. Yet the visits, now with my wife and two young daughters, continued. At the start of the 1970s, as a member of a progressive and busy natural history department in Birmingham, I began to make occasional pre-dawn field trips to the Midlands countryside, including the Cotswolds as far as Woodchester. The purpose of such trips was to obtain photographs for lectures and exhibitions, to heave rock specimens from working quarries for a new geology gallery, and to make contacts with real country craftsmen who could nurture the department's latest venture – Birmingham Nature Centre. It was at this time that I decided to visit Woodchester regularly, in my own time, often with the family, and to document its natural history in film and log; and so it has continued to the present day.

Each member of the natural history department had one or more special interests: mine included solitary bees and honey bees, foxes, badgers and weasels, and – particularly – stoats. Over many years, I accumulated such a fund of data on this most elusive of small predators that I began to wonder if I could put it to more than academic use. Esoteric scientific papers are all very well, but I wanted to record what I had learnt in a way that would appeal to young and old alike. I also wanted to indulge my love for the English language, and to combine my specific observations of stoats with my wider knowledge of Woodchester's local and natural history. Eventually, after a protracted gestation of 30 years, the idea crystallised: I would describe what I knew in narrative form. The result is a book – to be published in January – that is somewhere between science and fiction: an ecological narrative of 83,000 words based on the natural history and human history of Woodchester and its neighbouring parishes in Longtree Hundred. Called *Hunters of Longtree: A Cotswold Tale*, it is set at the start of the 1950s against a landscape

untouched by modern farming methods or myxomatosis, and describes the lives of predators such as stoat, weasel, otter, badger, fox, bats, and birds of prey – not in the anthropomorphised fictional form of, for example, *Watership Down*, but simply as a re-creation on paper of events that have actually occurred. I suppose the idea is that the reader should feel the same sort of emotions of fascination or excitement on seeing these events described as I and others have felt on actually observing them.

The main theme is the natural history of the stoat, the so-called 'royal hunter', and the book relates the stoat's territorial, hunting and reproductive behaviour in some detail. As a biologist, I am familiar with virtually every aspect of the stoat's natural history that has been record-ed by zoologists and naturalists (including me) over the past 150 years, and much of this information finds its way into the narrative in one form or another. Thus the book details the hazardous life of a female stoat and the for-tunes of her seven young over one year, from birth to inde-pendence and adulthood. The mother's maternal

Left to right, The Dark Wood, The Trough in Water Lane, Sunrise Over Longtree and The Dingle

behaviour and the young stoats' development are syn-
chronised with the seasonal behaviour and daily activity
rhythms of rabbits, voles, and other prey and their predators, the nesting behaviour of birds, the emergence and
life cycles of insects, the flowering of wild plants, and daily
human activities. Key characters in the fictionalised 'stoat
story' are named after personalities associated with
Woodchester's Anglo-Saxon past: but the point of it all is
that, for all the fictionalised dressing, it is *true*.

The Anglo-Saxon connection runs as a thread throughout the narrative. Two Anglo-Saxon charters for
Woodchester, relating to ownership of woodland in the
area, are among the earliest known: these on their own
became a fascinating and intriguing aspect of background
research. Woodchester lies in the Anglo-Saxon hundred of
Longtree, which is said to derive its name from a tall tree
that stood in the neighbouring parish of Avening. Under
the shelter of this tree the men of the tithing (one tenth of
a hundred) held their council; rather like a parish council
meeting today. Longtree could be said to be the key to my
ecological reconstruction, for the woodland of Woodchester provides the habitat of the animals depicted.

Hence this description of one of the main beech woods
there, which is the setting for the introduction of several of
the animals/characters: "The beech wood, through which
ran the northern boundary of Woodchester, was called
Dark Wood, which had grown up on an ancient rabbit
warren. A tawny owl hooted and huddled closer to an ivy-
clad beech bole to try to escape the attention of mobbing
titmice... In a burrow beneath its roots a dog stoat stirred
from his sleep. Sensing the warm sunshine outside, he
crawled along the short tunnel to the entrance and cau-

tiously peered out through bright, black eyes. This royal hunter, as the stoat is known in some parts of the world, we will call Aethelwald, which in the language of the Anglo-Saxons means 'noble and famous one'."

A tree is the site for the den of the female stoat, Gytha, who is about to give birth after being impregnated by Aethelwald the previous spring: "In her den in the alder tree hollow Gytha felt her young stir within her, and once more she licked the tight, tender skin of her swollen belly... She licked the moist, inflamed entrance to her birth canal, and in the time it took the barn owl to swallow another shrew, she gave birth to her first kitten... The kitten was barely larger than a filbertnut, coral-pink, and sparsely covered with short, white hairs, as delicate and downy as those growing along the edge of a young beech leaf when it has just burst from its winter bud in May."

Is this a valid way for a naturalist to 'write up' his observations? I don't know. But it does seem to me that, unless one attempts to create a sense of what a natural phenomenon would actually have been *like*, one is leaving out something important. The same could be said, I think, for the writing up of other observations. If you take a walk along Water Lane on a hot summer's day, you may quench your thirst at a sandstone water trough set in the high bank. Sadly, in recent years, the trough has been broken by a vehicle crashing into it, but it still holds some cool, clear water, which issues from a spring on the hillside above. Here is the trough in *The Hunters of Longtree*: "For many years the old drinking trough had been a wateringplace for farm-horse and human alike. Even during the driest of summers it was never empty, and it always provided a welcome sight to the weary walker... No one could say how old the trough was, or when it was set in the bank, or whether its water had been used to quench the thirst of woolpack horses and drovers treading this ancient way between Bath and Gloucester."

Almost opposite the entrance to Water Lane stands a white house with a modified drystone cattle pound, used to park cars: this is Larchgrove Cottage, now much enlarged and modernised, and not the same cottage I knew. Instead of providing space for cars, the pound used to house my aunt's chickens: "During the whole of her married life Lilian had kept and reared her own chickens in the pound. Throughout the recent war, she had never been short of eggs, and because her hens laid more during the year than she and her husband could use, she preserved some, for winter – when they would go off lay – in a pail of water-glass that she kept in a corner of her cool, walk-in pantry, alongside her home-made wine and ginger beer."

I remember my aunt mentioning the badger that regularly came down the road at night past the cottage and nosed around the entrance gate to the pound. She knew that given half a chance it would satisfy its liking for her hens' eggs. In those days there was no known connection between badgers and bovine TB. Badgers were not so plentiful then, and they posed no apparent threat to the cows that were kept by farmer Fawkes. The rich, raw milk from Fawkes's farm was something to be savoured, the like of which I will never taste again.

In 1951, the famous Woodchester Roman pavement, buried beneath the old churchyard, opened for the first time since 1935. It was reported in the Stroud News and Journal: "Mr Robert Henriques, writing in *The Field* last week, said, 'The best bob's worth in 30 years'." At that opening, I remember farmer Fawkes using full-cream milk from a churn to give a polish to the excavated mosaic. I also remember one of my Woodchester mates giving me some of the tesserae that he had retrieved from the excavated spoil. He knew of my fascination for 'fossils' and other 'old things'. He was lucky to have escaped the attention of the custodians of the pavement. My uncle was one of the nightwatchmen who slept on site (as he had also done in 1935 and 1926), to prevent pilfering.

During my researches into Woodchester's history, I discovered that the organiser of the two earlier digs, Edward Tuppen Wise, was the previous owner of Larchgrove Cottage and a bosom friend of A.E. Housman, who had been a visitor to Woodchester throughout his life. Housman's grandfather was the rector of Woodchester, and his godmother was Edward's mother.

The Old Priory, an Elizabethan mansion next to the old churchyard, becomes a stage for the action of one of the stoats in my book; this time a yearling dog stoat who infringes on the territory of the dominant stoat Aethelwald: "Through one of the open windows came the sound of children's laughter. As he galloped across the lawn, the stoat stopped and cocked his head at the little girl who came running from the house. The child called to her sister to come and see the beautiful creature in the garden. But she had hardly uttered her cries of delight, when the stoat vanished into the shadow of the high stone wall that separated the garden from the old churchyard." It was in a place I knew as the Dingle that I first remember seeing stoats in Woodchester: they were hunting over the rabbit warrens, when rabbits were numerous, a few years before man introduced myxomatosis to control their number. This had an effect on the whole ecology of Woodchester, as in the rest of the countryside. Foxes, badgers, stoats and weasels, even otters, and buzzards were suddenly deprived of a reliable, high-energy food source, and their numbers declined for a long period, and led to less human-friendly eating habits.

The decimation of the rabbit population also had a harmful effect on the populations of beautiful blue butterflies living on the limestone grassland of the area, particularly the Adonis Blue and the extremely rare Large Blue. The Large Blue eventually became extinct; this was due to the lack of grazing by rabbits to produce a short turf, which was essential for the survival of the ants that enabled the completion of the butterfly's life cycle. The ants' nests became too shaded from the life-giving sun, and the ants had difficulty foraging in the dense herbage; wild thyme, the food plant of the butterfly's larva, also failed to thrive. Recent attempts in the area to reintroduce the butterfly have so far failed.

During the early 1950s you would have been lucky to see a stoat performing its so-called 'dance of death" on the rabbit-infested hillside of the Dingle. I have been lucky enough to witness this, though not in Woodchester, which is why I have included it among the many accounts of stoats' hunting behaviour that occur throughout the narrative. This one involves Aethelwald: "Other rabbits joined those already transfixed by his capers. He continued to dash around in ever widening circles, until he passed almost within springing distance of several rabbits, who crouched motionless, mesmerised by this strange behaviour. Suddenly, he stopped in mid-circuit and began to dance around on his hindlegs, with his forepaws held up like a begging dog. As he pranced past one unsuspecting rabbit, he turned in his tracks and leapt on its back, his jaws soon finding the vulnerable spot between the first two vertebrae of its skinny neck. Before the rabbit felt the stoat's fangs, its screams broke the bewilderment of the rest of the colony, and they rushed for their holes at the edge of Dark Wood, while Aethelwald gorged himself on his kill."

Generally our so-called civilised society has become divorced from such natural events as predation, though we sometimes see a sanitised version of it on our televisions. People think of it as 'cruel' – a term which only has any relevance when man deliberately inflicts pain on an animal. Such thinking fails to understand that all Nature is – in Tennyson's phrase – "red in tooth and claw" and that predation has been the key to the survival of species since long before the age of dinosaurs. As for cruelty: that hunt is Aethelwald's last before being run down by a speeding car on the main Bath Road.

There are also instances where the royal hunter – in this case one of Aethelwald's offspring, young Aethelbeorht – appears as a seemingly benign creature: "Lilian, who like many true country folk had a way with wild creatures, seemed to instil trust in the young stoat, for Aethelbeorht placed his other forepaw on her shoe and began to lick the soft calf leather. She froze, fascinated by the boldness of the beautiful creature with the glossy coat and dark, appealing eyes, and marvelled at the lithe movements of its limbs, whose touch she barely felt. She watched the inquiring face with alert ears constantly twitching, their parchment-thin linings a delicate, translucent pink and fringed with fine, pale golden hairs. She saw too the brown velvety muzzle sprouting long, sensitive whiskers, and the moist brown nose with ever-dilating and contracting nostrils. But most alluring of all were those dark, piercing, slightly bulbous eyes."

These fleeting glances at *Hunters of Longtree* would be incomplete without a mention of foxhunting. At around the age of eight I had my first glimpse of a fox in woodland, on a frosty morning. It was a dog fox in full winter coat. I was with my father, a keen foot follower of foxhounds. I have never forgotten that magical moment. Over the years, as an occasional foot follower, I have quizzed huntsmen and masters of hunts, especially the Berkeley, to satisfy my curiosity about the sport. I have been more interested in the behaviour of hounds and the hunted fox – natural predator and prey – than in that of the field.

Woodchester Park, in which an unfinished mansion stands, used to be a venue for the Berkeley many years ago. This extract describes the end of a hunt (which began in neighbouring Nympsfield) in the park: "Diplomat was turning short with his quarry and running hard at his brush. When within only a few bounds of Kennel Pond and the safety of its reedy margin, the fox felt a blow on his flank as the heavy hound crashed into him, winding him and knocking him off his feet. Lying on his back, he lunged at Diplomat with jaws snapping wildly. He saw the hound's bloodshot eyes and great jaws open wide, but hardly felt their powerful and fatal grip round his neck.

"In an instant the fox went limp and the pack began to break up his corpse, so that by the time the huntsman arrived to find the hounds' muzzles smeared with blood, only one of his pads, his brush, and part of his mask remained. The huntsman sounded several sharp, tremulous blasts on his horn to tell the field that the hounds had made a kill. Near the very same spot in the park Berkeley Nathan had killed a fox more than a century before."

Nostalgia is a natural element of human nature, and I do not deny that nostalgia has had its part to play in the creation of my 'Cotswold tale'. But it is not supposed to be backward-looking; it is simply a real-life drama of survival in the countryside. My purpose in publishing my experiences of Longtree is not to retreat into the past; rather, it is to share with others a privileged knowledge of a part of the English countryside that, inevitably, has changed over the past 50 years. As a biologist I realise the inevitability of change in animal and plant communities. So too must human communities and their environments change.

To return after a long absence to a place which one knew as a child, and of which one has happy memories, can be a sobering and disappointing experience. However, to return repeatedly to that same place over many years, from the years of youth to those of grandparenthood, is quite another thing and can reasonably be described as 'the experience of a lifetime'. Rather than find disappointment on my numerous returns to Woodchester, I have found nothing but pleasure during my quest.

Hunters of Longtree – A Cotswold Tale, *by David Walker, illustrated by the author's own wood engravings, will be published in the New Year. (Orpheus Press, £18).*

ANNALISA BARBIERI

The confessions of a fishing correspondent

WHO EVER THOUGHT I'D END UP IN LOVE WITH FISH? NOT me. For years I never gave them a thought. I had a goldfish as a child (Jimmy) who was exterminated because he ate the bulgy eyes of the exotic fish that shared his tank. Fish and me: there wasn't much of a connection. I didn't even eat fish and chips until I was thirty and found myself on the beach in Hastings with a new and incredulous boyfriend who'd spotted a fish and chip shop. They were delicious.

It was not long after that that I picked up a fly rod for the first time. I thought myself adept at casting, practising on the lawn. "This is like a big long whip," I thought, "I can do this." What happy ignorance. A few days later the rod and I were in a boat on a little lake in Bedfordshire. I was standing up, not at all what you should do in a boat. My boyfriend, the same one from Hastings beach and a fine fisherman, was tutoring me. "When the fish bite it's like having an electric shock." Within seconds I was plugged in, panicked and handing the rod over to him. I had never seen an animal fighting for its life and it was humbling and terrifying. I sat in the boat and cried. This, I thought, will turn me not into a fisherman, but a vegetarian. After half an hour, however, I was back in position and this time when the trout took my fly, a little green and black Montana, I played him in. He was a rainbow trout, not indigenous to these isles but the 'housewife's choice'. She, apparently, prefers its pink flesh on a plate to the white one of our true native trout: the brown. Not that I'd ever given any of this much thought before. I didn't kill my trout then, because I didn't know what to do, so my boyfriend handled that. But that evening I took my harvest home to my parents' house and presented him to my father. It's important to know that he is Italian and I have no brothers. I was the hunter gatherer now.

My boyfriend warned me that it wasn't usually that easy. I, with the false confidence of one who tastes success too easily, disputed this. "I'm a natural," I quietly told myself. This was about April, six years ago. We went fishing many more times that year and, if I'd had any prowess that first outing, I progressively lost it as I became less and less able to cast. I never knew I had such capacity for tantrums, and when the tears flowed, they were hot with frustration. I stamped with such ferocity on the river bank there were reports of crop circles in the places where I'd been. I had a birthday. I got a rod, a Shakespeare Expedition Fly (still my favourite, and most used rod) and a reel. My kit was starting to grow.

January. I attended a press trip to Scotland to write a travel piece. It was to be a journey of many firsts: fishing for salmon on the opening day of the Tay; meeting Ally Gowans, creator of the most deadly salmon fly in the last decade: the Ally's Shrimp; the tasting of several fine sin-gle-malts; haggis; a ceilidh. It was, too, my first time in Scotland. When Ally called for volunteers to make an Ally's Shrimp under his supervision, my hand shot up with a keenness never shown at school. The fly I made was perfect. Of course, I wanted very much to please.

The fusion of so many of the lovely things that sur-round fishing stayed with me. I still remember that feeling of coming back from salmon fishing all day, feeling tired in a way I'd long forgotten. A deep, physical fatigue not felt since childhood, after an honest day's play; not the mental exhaustion of adulthood. My bath that night, after the fishing but before the ceilidh and haggis and whisky, was the best bath I've ever had.

The next month I was having a conversation with Rosie Boycott, then editor of both *The Independent* and *The Independent on Sunday*. I can't remember how fishing came up; probably I was trying to distract from something Rosie had asked me that I didn't know the answer to. But when I mentioned fishing she exploded with excitement; appar-ently, she too fished. Whatever we'd just been talking about was forgotten as all chatter turned to fishing – this is what always happens when fishermen find each other. "Write about it," she said. And, with the approval of the sports editor, Paul Newman, I started to write a fishing column for the daily paper, every other Saturday. And thus it has been ever since.

The first one, about a recent trip to the Teviot, was not very good. It was jargony and trying too hard to be some-thing it wasn't. But soon, the column found its feet. I wanted to capture what it was that I loved about fishing, which wasn't just the fishing. Because fly fishing was what I'd started off doing, that was what I mostly wrote about. But on that trip to Scotland I'd met a man called Mick and his wife Kathie. Mick worked for the Angling Times and once held the record for the biggest pike ever caught in the UK. We stayed in touch.

Back in London, I went about introducing myself to the fishing industry. I should mention that at the time I was also contributing editor of the Independent on Sunday, a vague title that I'd insisted on to cover up the fact that I edited the fashion pages and wrote a fashion advice column called 'Dear Annie'. My notebook was becoming schizophrenic: alongside sketches from the fashion shows

were line drawings showing the life cycle of a mayfly.

If anyone in the fishing world was surprised to see a girl writing about fishing, they didn't show it, although I noticed a few of them spoke very quickly, and were unnecessarily technical in their explanations. At times I did (and still, occasionally, do) feel lost, and stupid and a fraud. Unlike most people that write about fishing, I am a writer first and a fisherman second. Luckily, I had a splendid boyfriend at home who could answer the questions that were really stupid. But I was learning. Writing about fishing, however, meant that I had to have something to write about. And although I was insistent that the column wouldn't just be about me fishing (which I think is incredibly boring), I did have to make sure I actually went fishing. And sometimes this meant freezing on the side of a river fishing for grayling in February (this is how I spent one very happy Valentine's day), wondering: why? But then I'd catch a beautiful fan-finned grayling, it would get off, and I would spend all evening thinking about his silvery beauty whilst I thawed out with a steak and kidney pie. I'd think about the take, the playing in, the loss, the what-might-have-been.

Days like this were balanced out by days of heat and sun, lovely picnics and watching damselflies curve their cobalt-blue backs in mating. Three things were starting to surprise me. How much I loved the fish: I was starting to learn some wonderful things about them from the many books I had begun to amass. How much I loved the insects! They were no longer just buzzy things – I could pick out olives, stoneflies, hawthorns and, of course, fat juicy mayflies. I dredged the river bed with fishing and fly-tying supremo Oliver Edwards to learn about all stages of bug life. (How proud I was one day when my boyfriend – who had been fishing for 15 years before me – asked what a cased caddis looked like and, under my instruction, was soon able to tie an imitation of one which, the very next day, caught fish.) And, thirdly, how much I loved the picnics. I'd often start nibbling from the picnic basket as soon as we got to the river's edge. I grew quite satisfied.

My introduction to coarse fishing came courtesy of Mick, whom I still rely on for coarse fishing tuition, kit and delicious hospitality. Our first trip was in January, exactly a year after first meeting and we fished for pike. Coarse fishing was a revelation: there was so much kit! And you got to sit down and eat crisps, not at all like fly fishing where you move about and cast and cast until your arm drops off. He's since introduced me to many other species. One boiling hot day in July a few years later, with Mick refusing all my offers of sun cream, I caught four new-to-me fish: carp, rudd, tench and a roach.

The casting, after two years and cadging tuition from whomever I could (fortuitously this included some of the world's best), improved until I could present a dry fly to a fish rising under an overhanging branch with the delicacy of a mother placing her new-born down to sleep. But spey casting for salmon was a different story. Despite the attentions of people like Michael Daunt, of the Hugh Falkus School of Spey Casting, this still has some way to go. Although a great part of my fishing is very ordinary – I go to day ticket waters just like every one else (and, yes, I pay) – I do also like to stick my nose into other aspects of fishing. Because I still have a newcomer's curiosity, I think everyone else *must* be as fascinated as I am to know how a rod is made, the journey a salmon makes to spawn, what makes a brown trout run away to sea and become a sea trout (no one knows). I fish mostly in the UK, with the odd foray to Madeira for marlin (none were caught) and the Arno in Florence for carp.

Slowly, the paraphernalia in the fishing shops started to make sense. You know when you first start a job and everyone is just a sea of faces, but then as the weeks pass people become personalities and everything comes into focus? So it was with fishing. But because I was – and am – relatively new to it compared to the 'man and boy' fish-ermen I meet, I can understand the frustration and confu-sion of the non-angler too. My proudest feedback is when I get emails saying "I don't fish, but I read your column..."

One day, I decided to fuse fashion and fishing. Within the fashion industry, because I talked about fishing non-stop, I found out that there were people that also fished: the designer John Rocha was one. So too the man who makes things in leather: Bill Amberg. And men's shoe designer Oliver Sweeney (with whom I went fishing to Florence). With a couple of others I had them photo-graphed for the fashion pages as 'Fashion people that fish'. I was nervous of my editor's reaction (by this stage Rosie had long since gone); luckily he loved it. But soon, the fashion and fishing calendars started to clash. I was need-ed at shows just as the trout season was opening, the best sea trout fishing was to be had just as Paris fashion week was starting. Eventually, I handed the fashion pages over to my deputy, and left to go freelance, and to be free to fish just as much as I wanted. Sometimes I fish every couple of days (on holidays in Devon I only seem to take my waders off to sleep), sometimes not for several weeks. There's much more to fishing than the catching of fish.

It's now nearly six years since I first picked up a rod. (I did fish in Italy, as a child, using freshly caught crickets as bait, but that doesn't really count as we never caught anything and I'm not entirely sure what we were fishing for.) I'm now confident enough in most situations to follow my instinct, often quite against advice. It's not that I think I know better, but I like to find things out for myself. I only possess three rods: my beloved Shakespeare Expedition, a 7ft rod for Dartmoor streams and a salt-water rod, the newest addition which I hope will see a bit more action than it has, even though I am afraid of the sea. I have two pairs of wellingtons, lined for winter, unlined for summer. My waders I waited some years for (women's sized waders were not easy to come by), once traipsing across Toronto in the hope that the North Americans might be more advanced (they weren't). In the end I found them in Pall Mall. Fishing talk is second nature to me. Just as I slide from Italian to English and back again without noticing, so I talk 'fish'. Did I ever not know about the magical world that exists beyond the water's edge? Did I ever really live any other way?

DUFF HART-DAVIS

The Beasts of Britain

THE IDEA OF WRITING AN ENCYCLOPAEDIA ABOUT THE
creatures of the kingdom did not burst on me suddenly:
rather, it grew over many years, as, in the course of
research for other books and articles in magazines and
newspapers, I gradually extended my knowledge of
wildlife and farming. The more I wrote about the countryside, the more clearly I realised that, even in our crowded
little islands, densely settled by 60 million people, we have
an astonishing variety of fauna, both wild and domesti-
cated. Foreign trips – to India, Africa and Siberia, among
other destinations – helped put our own conservation
problems into perspective. Our efforts to encourage the
dormouse, for instance, seem microscopic in comparison
with the Indian Government's attempt to save the tiger.
But who is to say that diminutive rodents do not deserve
the best assistance we can give them? Visits to Ascension
Island in the South Atlantic graphically showed me the
folly of introducing exotic species into environments

which have no native animals to control them. Cats, taken to Ascension in the 1820s to keep down the rats, preferred to eat seabirds, went wild, and remain a nuisance to this day – and so, in exactly the same way, grey squirrels brought to England from North America in the 1860s to 'brighten up' our fauna, have proved an immensely expensive menace to forestry.

It was never my intention to produce a dry textbook restricted to facts and figures. I wanted all along to include folklore and superstition – for example about black cats, which have been seen as harbingers of both good and bad luck – and I was anxious to bring in some history, not only of the animals and birds themselves, but also of our ancestors' attitudes towards them. Enjoying research, I delved into early authors, among them Julius Caesar, whom I remembered from schooldays giving a ridiculous account of the elk. Sure enough, there in *De Bello Gallico* is the general's authoritative statement that the elk has no joints in its legs, so that it cannot lie down, and has to sleep leaning against trees. To capture it, all the wily hunter need do is note which trees the elk favours, and privily cut almost through the trunks: thus, when the elk comes along for a nap, over goes the tree, and the animal with it. In England, ignorance of this kind persisted into the 17th century, when Edward Topsell published his *Historie of Four-Footed Beastes*, the first comprehensive account of exotic animals in English. His descriptions of elephant and rhinoceros were tolerably accurate, but he also fully believed in the existence of unicorns, and of the lamia, a kind of terrestrial mermaid, with scaly body, claws on front feet and cloven hoofs behind, who lured men into range by flashing her comely breasts.

More accurate knowledge came slowly. That wonderfully patient observer Gilbert White published his *Natural History and Antiquities of Selborne* in 1789 – yet even a man as learned as Samuel Johnson (1709-81) believed that swallows disappeared in winter because they 'conglobulated' into large masses and spent the cold months hibernating on the beds of rivers.

For me, one major difficulty was the need to be selective. My publishers set a limit for the text of 180,000 words, and it was clear from the start that I could not possibly mention every creature that now exists, or has existed, in Britain and Ireland. Mammals presented no problem, for we have relatively few; but what was I to do about

birds, of which some 550 species frequent the United Kingdom? If all were described and illustrated, they alone would more than fill the space available. Insects, with over 100,000 species present, presented a still more formidable challenge. The only sensible solution seemed to be to include those species which people were most likely to have come across – to have read about or seen on television – and those which, for various reasons, have recently been causing concern. Into this last category come songbirds, whose decline has been making newspaper headlines for the past 30 years, and also badgers, whose apparent ability to transmit tuberculosis to cattle has made them the centre of acrimonious controversy.

Above all, I wanted the book to be realistic, and to reflect my belief that mankind should manage wildlife in the same practical way that farmers manage domestic stock. In an introduction I explained that I was brought up on a remote farm on the Chilterns and spent every school holiday in the company of a gamekeeper, going the rounds of his snares and traps, ferreting rabbits, shooting squirrels and lying in wait for foxes. I learnt that every day and night countless creatures are killing others in order to survive: I saw stoats doggedly hunting down rabbits, thrushes cracking open snails by battering them on stones, swallows hawking insects in mid-air, kestrels hovering to spot mice in the grass. Death, I realised, was as much a part of nature as life. I also saw that grey squirrels were destroying every young beech tree planted since World War II, by gnawing the bark in early summer, and that – in those days before the advent of myxomatosis – rabbits would devastate farm crops unless vigorous control measures were taken against them. So I became a hunter, and grew up in the belief that it is perfectly in order for humans to cull wildlife, either for purposes of pest-control, or for the pot, provided the job is carried out humanely. In those days the concept of conservation had scarcely been invented, and professional conservationists were as thin on the ground as corncrakes. Now they are everywhere as the growth of the Royal Society for the Protection of Birds graphically illustrates. Membership of the society accelerated progressively from 10,000 in 1960 to 100,000 in 1972, to 500,000 in 1989 and 1,000,000 in 1998. Tighter legislation – notably the Wildlife and Countryside Act of 1981 – has greatly increased protection for many species. Yet public concern, and the advocacy of individual conservationists, have also played a large part in giving wildlife a better deal. It was the publication of Rachel Carson's book *Silent Spring* in 1962 that first raised the alarm about the dangers of agricultural chemicals, and put a brake on the reckless poisoning of the environment.

Raptors, in particular, have achieved stirring comebacks – not least peregrine falcons, which have regained pre-war levels after declining to a low ebb in the 1950s and 1960s, when organochlorine compounds made the shells of their eggs unviably thin. Still more striking has been the success of the osprey, exterminated by gamekeepers in 1916, but now nesting again in England as well as in Scotland; and the return of the red kite, secretly reintroduced to the Chilterns in 1989 by the RSPB and English Nature. On a less spectacular level, bats, butterflies, hedgehogs and newts now get dedicated support from official and volunteer bodies, and on the farm front there is greater enthusiasm than ever for strengthening rare breeds of cattle, sheep, goats and horses.

Sometimes, however, conservation (in my view) can be carried to ridiculous lengths. Consider the question of geese on Islay, off the west coast of Scotland. In the old days the principal landowners on the island used to meet once a year, decide how many geese should be culled that winter, and shoot accordingly, thus maintaining reasonable control of the population at zero cost. When shooting was banned, the numbers of overwintering barnacle geese rose to more than 30,000 – a number which the farmers could not tolerate, as their grass was being either eaten or destroyed by a deluge of droppings. Scottish Natural Heritage has therefore been obliged to deploy a whole team of counters and scarers, and farmers are paid compensation for having geese on their land. In 2000-2001 the cost of the scheme – to taxpayers – was £637,000. In my view, it is only common sense to cull birds and animals whose numbers become excessive. Hardly anyone disputes the idea that as many rats as possible should be destroyed. But what about badgers? Every dairy farmer in the south-west of England would like to see them thinned out, but whenever the Government sets up an experimental cull, there is a tremendous outcry. Shepherds, poultry-keepers and the managers of bird reserves all hate foxes – yet Reynard has countless human friends, who stand up for him vociferously. Far too many people still think of grey squirrels as cuddly pets, and far too many have bambified ideas about deer.

The spread of deer has been one of the greatest wildlife changes during my lifetime. It seems strange, as Britain becomes ever more crowded, and more land disappears under concrete or asphalt, that deer numbers should be rocketing. And yet they are. In the Scottish Highlands the continual increase in the red deer herd to a total of more than 300,000 has been partly due to global warming and the lack of harsh winters, which used to kill off thousands of old or weak animals; but, further south, all five other species of deer (fallow, roe, sika, muntjac and Chinese water deer) are also flourishing, to such a degree that they constitute a severe threat to forestry. Muntjac, or barking deer, which originally escaped from the park at Woburn Abbey early in the 20th century, have now colonised much of England and are still on the increase, infuriating gardeners with their predilection for roses and runner beans. Part of the deer's success can be ascribed to the increase of ideal habitat in the form of new plantations – and woodland managers are uncomfortably aware that the spread of the extensive community forests now being planted is about to create a further huge deer problem.

Another major change has been the increase in road traffic, and in the speed at which people drive. The number of badgers killed on the roads every year is thought to be about 50,000: in other words, some 140 badgers are being run over every night, or one every five minutes. Foxes, although more agile, are no less vulnerable: at least 100,000 fall victim to vehicles annually. Owls also often become casualties, undone by their habit of hunting low along roads and verges in the dark. Toads are squashed in dreadful numbers when they move down to their mating ponds in spring – unless well-wishers have furnished them with tunnels through which they can pass safely beneath carriageways.

Yet the greatest change of all has been in the disposition of humans. Fifty years ago farms still employed relatively large numbers of workers; most forestry operations were conducted by hand or by horse; country businesses flourished, and the rural population remained fairly high. Today, with agriculture and timber-harvesting fully mechanised, there has been a mass withdrawal from the land, and 90 per cent of people live in towns and cities, where they are cut off from everyday contact with animals. This urbanisation seems to have created a new kind of 21st-century cruelty, manifest in the way owners abandon cats and dogs when they no longer want them. I find it appalling that people think it good enough to dump their pets in parks or fields and simply drive off, shutting their minds to the suffering they cause, and hoping that someone else will deal with the problem. Even horses are casually cast off in this way, and the country's numerous equine sanctuaries cannot answer anything like all the appeals for help.

For me, as a writer, the question was, how to put all these ideas and snippets of information together in book form? The problem was solved by Anthony Cheetham, founder and chief executive of the Orion publishing group, who had the experience and imagination to envisage a lavishly-illustrated encyclopaedia, and the resources to bring it into being. With the support of a first-class picture-researcher and editorial team, I spent much of the past year putting pieces of the jigsaw together. Because the text and pictures had to fit precisely, there was a good deal of last-minute fiddling. "Cut five lines from the belted Galloway cattle," Marilyn, my editor, would demand. "Add four lines about natterjack toads." Curses! What more, of general interest, was there to say about natterjacks?

By the time we heard that a rival *Fauna Britannica* was on its way, covering much the same ground and coming –

incredibly – from another firm in the same publishing group, it was too late to change course or title. All we could do was put our heads down and go for it. Now that the book is in being, I can only hope that people will get as much value and entertainment from reading it as I did from writing it – and if it inspires young people to join a body such as one of the Wildlife Trusts, or to volunteer for the bird-counts organised by the British Trust for Ornithology, I shall be delighted.

Fauna Britannica, *by Duff Hart-Davis, is published by Weidenfeld & Nicolson (£30).*

ALICE OSWALD

The voices on the Dart

For two years, Alice Oswald travelled the length of Devon's River Dart, talking to people who live and work on it. Then she wove her 'poetic census' into an extraordinary poem, Dart – a 'sound map' or 'songline' in which the voices of poacher, ferryman, sewage worker, milk worker, forester, swimmer and canoeist are interwoven with historic, mythic and ghostly voices as she follows the river from its moorland source to the sea. The result, as the following two extracts show, is a haunting evocation of one of England's most beautiful rivers.

Who's this moving alive over the moor?

An old man seeking and finding a difficulty.

Has he remembered his compass his spare socks
does he fully intend going in over his knees off the
    military track from Okehampton?

keeping his course through the swamp spaces
and pulling the distance around his shoulders

the source of the
Dart – Cranmere
Pool on
Dartmoor, seven
miles from the
nearest road

and if it rains, if it thunders suddenly
where will he shelter looking round
and all that lies to hand is his own bones?

tussocks, minute flies,
       wind, wings, roots

He consults his map. A huge rain-coloured wilderness.
This must be the stones, the sudden movement,
the sound of frogs singing in the new year.
Who's this issuing from the earth?

The Dart, lying low in darkness calls out Who is it?
trying to summon itself by speaking...

the walker
replies

An old man, fifty years a mountaineer, until my heart
    gave out,
so now I've taken to the moors. I've done all the walks,
    the Two
Moors Way, the Tors, this long winding line the Dart

this secret buried in reeds at the beginning of sound I
won't let go of man, under
his soakaway ears and his eye ledges working
into the drift of his thinking, wanting his heart

I keep you folded in my mack pocket and I've marked in red
where the peat passes are and the good sheep tracks

cow-bones, tin-stones, turf-cuts.
listen to the horrible keep-time of a man walking,
rustling and jingling his keys
at the centre of his own noise,

[140]

clomping the silence in pieces and I

I don't know, all I know is walking. Get dropped off the
military track from Oakenhampton and head down into
Cranmere pool. It's dawn, it's a huge sphagnum kind of
wilderness, and an hour in the morning is worth three in
the evening. You can hear plovers whistling, your feet
sink right in, it's like walking on the bottom of a lake.

What I love is one foot in front of another. South-south-
west and down the contours. I go slipping between Black
Ridge and White Horse Hill into a bowl of the moor
where echoes can't get out

listen,
a
lark
spinning
around
one
note
splitting
and
mending
it

and I find you in the reeds, a trickle coming out of a
    bank, a foal of a river

one step-width water
of linked stones
trills in the stones
glides in the trills
eels in the glides

in each eel a fingerwidth of sea

in walking boots, with twenty pounds on my back: spare
socks, compass, map, water purifier so I can drink from
streams, seeing the cold floating spread out above the
morning,

tent, torch, chocolate, not much else.

Which'll make it longish, almost unbearable between my
evening meal and sleeping, when I've got as far as stopping, sitting in the tent door with no book, no saucepan,
not so much as a stick to support the loneliness

he sits clasping his knees, holding his face low down
   between them,
he watches black slugs,
he makes a little den of his smells and small thoughts
he thinks up a figure far away on the tors
waving, so if something does happen,
if night comes down and he has to leave the path
then we've seen each other, somebody knows where
   we are.

falling back on appropriate words
turning the loneliness in all directions...

       *   *   *

...shhh I can make myself invisible
with binoculars in moist places. I can see frogs
hiding under spawn – water's sperm – whisper, I wear
   soft colours

naturalist

whisper, this is the naturalist
she's been out since dawn
dripping in her waterproof notebook

I'm hiding in red-brown grass all different lengths, bog
bean, sundew, I get excited by its wetness, I watch spiders
watching aphids, I keep my eyes in crevices, I know two
secret places, call them x and y where the Large Blue
Butterflies are breeding, it's lovely, the male chasing the
female, frogs singing lovesongs

she loves songs, she belongs to the soundmarks of larks

I knew a heron once, when it got up
its wings were the width of the river,
I saw it eat an eel alive
and the eel the eel chewed its way back inside out
   through the heron's stomach
like when I creep through bridges right in along a ledge
   to see where the dippers nest.
Going through holes, I love that, the last thing through
   here was an otter

(two places I've seen eels, bright whips of flow
like stopper waves the rivercurve slides through
trampling around at first you just make out
the elver movement of the running sunlight
three foot under the road-judder you hold
and breathe contracted to an eye-quiet world

by the bridge, an
eel watcher

while an old dandelion unpicks her shawl
and one by one the small spent oak flowers fall
then gently lift a branch brown tag and fur
on every stone and straw and drifting burr
when like a streamer from your own eye's iris
a kingfisher spurts through the bridge whose axis
is endlessly in motion as each wave
photos its flowing to the bridge's curve
if you can keep your foothold, snooping down
then suddenly two eels let go get thrown
tumbling away downstream looping and linking
another time we scooped a net through sinking
silt and gold and caught one strong as bike-chain
stared for a while then let it back again
I never pass that place and not make time
to see if there's an eel come up the stream
I let time go as slow as moss, I stand
and try to get the dragonflies to land
their gypsy-coloured engines on my hand)

whose voice is this who's talking in my larynx
who's in my privacy under my stone tent
where I live slippershod in my indoor colours
who's talking in my lights-out where I pull to
under the bent body of an echo are these your
fingers in my roof are these your splashes...

Dart, *by Alice Oswald (from which these extracts are taken),
is published by Faber & Faber, £8.99*